CONTENTS

PART ONE

PART TWO

✓ ***"Who lies for you will lie against you" – Bosnian Proverb***

✓ ***"We lie loudest when we lie to ourselves" - Eric Hoffer***

PART ONE

INTRODUCTION

Although we are surrounded with more access to information than has ever been known before we are also surrounded by more misinformation. With TV, radio, newspapers and the internet all commonplace and readily available at our fingertips to inform and educate us every minute of the day or night we are also subject to more scams, lies, rumours and deception.

Throughout history there have been some really enormous frauds, false scientific claims, downright lies and subterfuge but on the whole these were isolated cases and, before modern media, were very localised. Lots of these claims could not be confirmed or denied until centuries later when we had more modern thinking, sophisticated science and technology. At the time, however, without the help of such modern technology and science, these claims were met with great astonishment and belief.

According to the Bible the very history of man began with Eve and the serpent's lie and deceit has been with us ever since. No matter what the place, ideology or religion people have schemed and plotted to deceive others to make money or gain positions of power. Over the centuries man seems to have been uniquely willing to believe almost anything, never having learnt the lessons of the past.

✓ ***"The ability to lie is a liability" - Unknown***

The Internet in particular, whilst a source of unlimited information is also the source of the greatest lies and scams of all time. Although it has the ability to disprove false claims it has, unfortunately, the vast ability to create new ones. People pretending to be who they are not, schemes to extract money from innocent victims, hoaxes and the like, not to mention confidence tricks and forgery, the internet has them all.

With all deception being based on a lie the most obvious place to start any book about any of the above would be to look at "the lie" in detail.

It would be impossible to include in one book all the scams, frauds and deceptions which have occurred over the centuries but the following should give just a small taster of some of the most famous ones.

✓ ***"The hardest tumble a man can make is to fall over his own bluff" - Ambrose Bierce***

LYING

It seems incredible, if not a little daunting, to think that there are about 20 different ways of lying (see pages 12-19). Although the origin of the word lie can be traced back to Middle English in 900AD, St. Augustine, a philosopher and theologian, composed a rather extensive writing on the subject in 396AD.

So what is a lie? In the Collins English Dictionary a lie is described as "to speak untruthfully with intent to mislead or deceive, to convey a false impression or practise deception".

Another dictionary describes a lie as "a type of deception in the form of an untruthful statement with the intention to deceive, often with the further intention to maintain a secret or reputation, to protect someone's feelings from getting hurt, or to avoid punishment."

Lying is usually associated with a falsehood in an oral or a written context although, as we shall see, there are many forms of deception such as forgeries, fraud and hoaxes.

A lie, which can also be called a prevarication, a falsehood or duplicity, is an intention to deceive others. Lies frequently assume "lives of their own" and result in consequences that people do not intend or fail to predict.

✓ ***"Truth is not determined by majority vote" – Doug Gwyn***

There can be two consequences of lying, either the lie is discovered or it remains undiscovered.

The discovery of a lie can, in many instances, undermine everything else the speaker says and can even lead to legal sanctions against the speaker, as in the case of perjury. The person who uncovers the lie could, in certain circumstances be dragged into the lie and be coerced into collaborating with the liar and become part of a conspiracy. They in turn could actively tell the lie to other people.

Although, as mentioned previously, there are 20 different types of lies, fortunately, all lies are not created equal. St. Augustine, the philosopher and theologian who greatly influenced the development of Western Christianity, for instance, believed that there were only nine categories of lying, several of which could be classified as white lies. These are lies which make the world go round for example, a lie which rather than harm someone, does in fact help - such as when we tell a friend, who is perhaps not looking very well after a long illness, that they look absolutely wonderful.

Sir Walter Scott, (pictured right) the famous Scottish historical novelist and poet wrote in the 1800's – "Oh, what a tangled web we weave when first we practice to deceive!" This tangled web describes the often difficult procedure of covering up a lie so that it is not detected in the future.

✓ ***"With lies you may get ahead in the world, but you can never go back" - Russian proverb***

In his paper "Human, All Too Human", the philosopher Friedrich Nietzche does in fact suggest that many people try not to lie only because they cannot maintain the lie. He suggests that lying divides people into categories of strength and ability to maintain a lie so that some people only tell the truth because they are too weak to maintain a lie.

Sisella Bok in her book "Lying: Moral Choice in Public and Private Life", looks at the effects of deception on individuals and society in general. Witten in 1978 the book won the George Orwell Award and the Melcher Book Award and is still in print today.

In his book "The Politics of Lying: Implications for Democracy" Lionel Cliffe looks at the secrecy and deception of those in power whilst Peter Oborne in his book "The Rise of Political Lying" traces the history of political lying back to its origins (see page 139).

So what, then, is the truth about lying?

✓ ***"It does not require many words to speak the truth" - Chief Joseph, leader of the Tribe, Nez Perce.***

PSYCHOLOGY OF LYING

Bella DePaulo of the University of Virginia at Charlottesville, USA, has done several studies on lying and says "no one is totally honest all the time". In one of her studies, published in the Journal of Personality and Social Psychology, she revealed that the more socially adept amongst us stretch the truth more often than the less socially adept. In 1932 Jean Piaget, an eminent Swiss psychologist, wrote "The tendency to tell lies is a natural tendency, spontaneous and universal." This would seem especially so in what we call "a born liar."

It is something that wives and girlfriends have long suspected, and something which researchers have now revealed, that men are far more likely to tell lies than women!

Apparently a study of 3,000 adults for the researchers OnePoll has found that the average male (if there is such a thing!) tells roughly three lies a day. By contrast the average woman lies around twice a day. There is, however, a difference in the lies males and females tell – men revealed that their lies are mostly about their habits and they are less likely to feel guilty about their lying. Women on the other hand tend to lie about their feelings with such phrases as "No, there's nothing wrong with me, I'm fine", thus hiding their true feelings.

✓ ***"If any question why we died, tell them, because our fathers lied" - Rudyard Kipling***

Whilst women may tell fewer lies, 82% of females questioned said telling a lie ate away at their conscience, but only 70% of men confessed to pangs of guilt. Almost 75% of those taking part in the survey agreed it was OK to lie to save someone's feelings. Katie Maggs, Associate Medical Curator at the Science Museum, suggests that lying may seem to be an unavoidable part of human nature, saying that "...it's an important part of social interaction".

Women will also lie to friends about how an outfit looks in order to make themselves look better by comparison! Experts said that the findings show women are far more competitive than they pretend to be.

It has yet to be ascertained whether human quirks like lying are the result of genes, evolution or upbringing. A poll was released ahead of the launch of the revamped "Who Am I" gallery" at the Science Museum, in West London, in June 2010, which aimed to make sense of brain science, genetics and human behaviour. Accordingly it was found that we are most likely to spin a yarn to our mothers, with 25% of men and 20% of women admitting to this. By comparison, however, only 10% said they were likely to deceive their partners.

Sociologists suggest that almost all lies, certainly the most malicious ones, are motivated by self-interest. This is what is known as an adaptive lie, a lie to avoid punishment or to achieve gain. Sociologists observe this phenomenon in children as young as 4 years of age.

✓ ***"The Truth is heavy, therefore few care to carry it" – Anonymous***

One study has suggested that lying takes longer than telling the truth.

Interestingly, people with Parkinson's disease find it almost impossible to deceive others. This seems to indicate a link between being dishonest and the functioning of the frontal lobes of the brain.

Damage to the frontal lobes has been linked to anti-social behaviour ranging from dishonesty to violence. A team at the University of Pennsylvania state that monitoring the frontal lobe area of the brain shows when people are lying as apparently the frontal lobe is more active when people are lying.

In many instances a lie is told with the very best of intent. Sometimes, when trying to do the right thing in an awkward situation, perfect honesty may not always be the best thing. Certain situations demand compassion and respect. Yet many philosophical and religious traditions have long claimed that rarely, if ever, is a lie permissible.

The question often posed is, if you are asked an immoral question can you answer with a lie? For example, if at any time an enemy came looking for someone you were hiding, would you be permitted to lie in order to protect them.

Most people would say such a lie was an act of virtue but not the 18th century philosopher Immanuel Kant who argued that telling a lie was always morally wrong.

✓ ***"It is hard to believe that a man is telling the truth when you know that you would lie if you were in his place" – Henry Louis Mencken***

Kant (pictured below) was a German philosopher from Eastern Prussia and was one of the most influential thinkers of his time. He was primarily concerned with moral

philosophy and his absolute belief that it was wrong to lie, no matter what the context of the question or its consequences. Because of his belief, Kant would not have lied when asked by an enemy if he was hiding anyone. He would have been extremely cruel and turned in anyone he was hiding. With honesty like that, most people would prefer lying!

✓ ***"For the truth is always older than all the opinions men have held regarding it; and one should be ignoring the nature of truth if we imagined that the truth began at the time it came to be known" - Blaise Pascal***

LYING AND RELIGION

The Catholic theological definition of a lie is, "To deny others access to knowledge to which they are entitled." According to Catholic teaching a lie can never be allowed, although it has been accepted that a lie of necessity is permissible.

Although not actually using the word "lie", the Bible has the issue well and truly covered with the ninth commandment which states "Though shalt not bear false witness." (right – Moses with the Ten Commandments).

Throughout the Bible truth has been stressed as being so important that it is mentioned hundreds of times. When brought before Pontius Pilate, Jesus said "I came into the world to testify to the truth. Everyone on the side of truth listens to me." However, Pilate's cynical response was "What is truth?"

In the Old Testament there is the well known story of Rahab who, whilst providing shelter in her house for two Israelite spies, actually lied about this to the King's men in order to protect them. Later her life, and the lives of her family, were spared when Jericho was destroyed which some people have suggested would indicate that God approved of lying under certain conditions.

✓ "I worship God as Truth only" - Mahatma Gandhi

Buddhism also takes a very firm line about lying, one of its rules prohibiting the use of lying. Indeed part of the Eightfold Path, which is central to Buddhism, asks for "Right Speech" which is, in fact, more than just not lying, for whilst lying is considered to be against "Right Speech", Buddhism warns against thinking that there is only one truth.

Although the Hindu tradition has a similar belief there is no definite ban on lying in the Vedas – the texts which came from ancient India which are part of the oldest Sanskrit literature and are the oldest scriptures of Hinduism. Although the Vedas states that "untruth" must be avoided it puts the responsibility on the listener rather than the speaker.

Of all the major religions in the world it is Islam which seems to be the most forgiving when it comes to lying. Whilst acknowledging in a chapter of the Quran, the central religious verbal text of Islam, that lying is not desirable "And do not say that of which you have no knowledge" and "Truly Allah guides not one who transgresses and lies" there are situations under which Muhammad does seem to permit a lie.

The Muslim tradition states that Muhammad said "Lying is wrong, except in three things: the lie of a man to his wife to make her content with him; a lie to an enemy, for war is deception; or a lie to settle trouble between people." Islam also allows for a Muslim to lie to protect life and to conceal their own faith if this means that no useful purpose would be served by being open. Unlike Immanuel Kant (see page 9) a Muslim would be quite prepared to protect any kind of victim.

✓ ***"I am the way, the truth and the life" - John 14:6***

TYPES OF LIES

As mentioned in the introduction it seems incredible, if not a little daunting, to think that there are about 20 different ways of lying. On the other hand, however, it seems a very sad reflection that there only seems to be 4 types of truth. From the following you can see the different types of lie and what they mean:

Bluffing
When we bluff we pretend we have something, or are going to do something, which is not the case. Quite a few games are actually based on the ability to be good at bluffing and, in this context, it is not regarded as immoral as all the players in the game understand and have consented to this form of bluffing in advance.

An athlete can bluff by pretending to move to the right and then dodge to the left and a poker player bluffs when he tries to deceive other players that he is holding different cards to those he really holds. Everyone in the game, whether it is an athlete or a card player, knows and accepts that the bluff is a perfectly acceptable form of the game.

Barefaced lies
A barefaced (or bald-faced) lie refers to a brazen lie which is clearly obviously to those hearing it. The term dates back to the 17th century and refers to a face without whiskers. Businessmen in the 18th and 19th century commonly wore beards and could easily mask their facial expressions thus, a bald-faced or, in Great Britain, the more common phrase "barefaced liar", was a person who was an exceptionally good liar who could lie without the need to hide his face.

✓ ***"Lies never pay the toll" - Croatian Proverb***

Compliments and false reassurances

These are assurances which are made solely to please or reassure another person. “You look really nice in that” or “Don’t worry, everything will turn out well in the end.” Whilst not strictly true these remarks are intended to be a comfort to the recipient and are said for their benefit rather than benefit of the teller.

Contextual lies

A contextual lie gives someone a false impression for, although the truth has been told, it has been deliberately taken out of context to give a false impression. In the same way one can also tell the truth but tell it in such an exaggerated and sarcastic way, or in an offended tone, that although the truth has been spoken the listener is made to believe that the speaker did not mean what he said.

Deception

This is to mislead deliberately, whether it be propaganda, sleight of hand or concealment. There is also the case of self-deception. The whole point about deception and deceiving is that it is fully intended and not just a genuine mistake, it is in fact fraud. It can take any of five different forms – making up a lie; making an ambiguous statement; omitting information; exaggeration or an understatement.

Denial

Denial is to lie to oneself. Sigmund Freud put forward the theory that it is a defence mechanism in which a person rejects something which is too difficult to accept insisting that, against overwhelming evidence, something is true.

✓ ***“Live truth instead of professing it” - Elbert Hubbard***

Economical with the truth

This is a phrase commonly used as a euphemism for deceit and lying, by leaving out important facts and deliberately holding back relevant information. It usually describes using facts but not revealing too much information. It could convey an untrue version of events.

First known to have been used in the 18th century by the politician Edmund Burke it is mostly associated with Sir Robert Armstrong, the UK Cabinet Secretary, who used the phrase during the 1986 Australian "Spycatcher" trial which saw the government of the day trying to ban the publication of a book written by a former MI5 employee.

Emergency lies

An emergency lie could, in fact, be called a strategic lie when the truth may not be told because, for example, the teller wishes to protect another person. It could also be told as a temporary lie to a second person because of the presence of a third person.

Fabrication

Fabrication is an outright statement, told as a truth, and, although it may be possible or plausible, it is in fact an assumption for which there is no valid proof, for example, a person giving directions to someone when they don't actually know the way. Propaganda is also classified as a fabrication.

✓ ***"Make yourself an honest man, and then you may be sure there is one less rascal in the world" - Thomas Carlyle***

Jokes

Jokes are, of course, lies but they are understood by all and sundry to be jesting and are taken as nothing more than that. Obviously there are various ways of joking. There is the practical joke which is a hoax or a deception. A really complicated joke can be seen as story telling and, even though the story teller will insist they are telling the truth, they are telling no more than that, i.e. a story or a tall tale. In a way, although the truth is not being told it is a matter of opinion as to whether these are in fact "real lies." St Augustine (pictured right) believed that jokes were not lies. He in fact addressed the question of lying and classified lies into eight kinds which he listed in order of severity as follows:

St. Augustine's classification of lies:

1. Lies in religious teaching;
2. Lies that harm others and help no one;
3. Lies that harm others and help someone;
4. Lies told for the pleasure of lying;
5. Lies told to "please others in smooth discourse";
6. Lies that harm no one and that help someone;
7. Lies that harm no one and that save someone's life;
8. Lies that harm no one and that save someone's "purity".

✓ ***"Man can certainly keep on lying, but he cannot make truth falsehood. He can certainly rebel, but he can accomplish nothing which abolishes the choice of God" - Karl Barth***

Hyperbole

Hyperbole is really a case of stretching the truth. It means that there is a basis of truth in the statement but the truth has been stretched to make it appear more important than it really is.

Lying to children

Whilst not deliberately wanting to lie to children we often do so by using euphemisms. We tell children fairy stories and ask them to believe in Father Christmas and the Tooth Fairy. They for their part tell lies, also known as bragging, in order to build up a reputation for themselves. They can also be said to tell bare-faced lies, for example, a child who has chocolate all over his face and denies that he has not eaten the last piece of chocolate cake.

Out of date signage

This category of lie includes any sort of advertisement which still remains after the business concerned has ceased to trade. It also includes the use of old stationery which shows out of date information.

Lying by omission

By omitting to tell someone an important piece of information, and deliberately giving a misconception, is lying by omission. It also includes the failure to correct any pre-existing misconceptions. An example of this is when the seller of a car declares that the car has been serviced regularly but does not mention that a fault was reported at the last service. A prime example of lying by omission is propaganda which is aimed at influencing people by not telling them the full facts.

✓ ***"A half truth is a whole lie" - Yiddish Proverb***

Lying in trade

Luckily we are now largely protected from lying in trade by Consumer Protection laws but a lot of advertising still pushes the boundaries of advertising by hiding a lot of the details in the small print.

Lying through your teeth

There seems to be no excuse for this form of lying. It is simply lying face to face and is quite deliberate.

Misleading or Concealing

Although a misleading statement does not tell an outright lie, there is, nonetheless, the intention of getting someone to believe in an untruth. Concealing also has the intention of misleading.

Noble lie

A noble lie is often told to maintain law, order and safety. This originated with Plato, the classical Greek philosopher and mathematician who helped to lay the foundation of Western philosophy. He believed that the people who know the whole truth must protect that truth in order to convince those who do not know the whole story.

Perjury

Perjury is a crime. It is the act of lying or making a false statement in any form on a matter whilst under oath or affirmation in a court of law.

✓ ***"Honesty is the rarest wealth anyone can possess, and yet all the honesty in the world ain't lawful tender for a loaf of bread" - Josh Billings***

It is a crime because the witness has sworn to tell "the truth, the whole truth and nothing but the truth" and, for the credibility of the court to remain intact, the witness testimony must be relied on as truthful.

(right – The Old Bailey, London)

Puffery

Puffery is a really exaggerated claim, the sort of thing to be found in advertising and publicity announcements. Although advertising statements are unlikely to be strictly true, in many instances they cannot be proved false and, as a result, do not violate trade laws. Consumers are expected to know that it is not the absolute truth.

White lie

White lies, as with compliments, are often told in order to avoid giving offence and would cause only minor complications if uncovered. They are often told to avoid giving offense, to save someone's feelings or simply to be polite. Nearly everyone at some time or another has told a white lie, even those who profess never to have told a lie. The term "white lie" has been used since at least the 1700s.

✓ ***"I'm not upset that you lied to me, I'm upset that from now on I can't believe you" - Friedrich Nietzsche***

According to the Oxford English Dictionary the earliest the phrase appeared in print was 1741. White has always been the colour of innocence, righteousness, goodness, and purity so calling a lie "white" seemed to be the perfect way to separate small lies from the larger, darker lies which are told.

✓ ***"One of the world's greatest problems is the impossibility of any person searching for the truth on any subject when they believe they already have it." - Dave Wilbur***

LEARNING TO LIE

The capacity to lie develops quite early on in human development. The first milestone in lying seems to develop in human beings at about the age of 4 years of age when children begin to find that they can tell stories and lie very convincingly - this is known as Machiavellian intelligence.

Children soon learn from experience, even before they necessarily understand why it works, that telling a lie can avoid punishment, they are also capable of telling fantastic and unbelievable stories. They lack the experience to know whether a statement is believable as they do not understand the concept of believability, lies such as "My Daddy has the most expensive car in the world!" This is a lie which is known as bragging and is told in order to build up a reputation for themselves and they are often expressing things that they wish were true. And what about the child who has chocolate all over his face and denies that he has not eaten the last piece of chocolate cake? Children also lack the moral experience to know when to refrain from lying and it takes a long time to develop a proper understanding of lies and their consequences. They also love lies such as bluffing, story telling, exaggeration and jokes.

Far from being a sign of future problems, research has shown that children who tell lies from an early age are more likely to become high achievers in later life. It is claimed that the complex brain processes involved in formulating a lie are indicators of a toddler's intelligence.

✓ ***"Unlike grown ups, children have little need to deceive themselves" - Johann Wolfgang Von Goethe***

A study of 1,200 children found that a fifth of two year olds are likely to tell lies, rising to 90% from the age of four. As children reach the ages of 6-8 they begin to understand that lying is wrong. There are many reasons why children in this age group lie – they may want to avoid punishment, to impress others, to protect others, to get something they want, or, more importantly, – because they hear their parents lie! This figure increases further until children reach their lying peak at 12. However, this tendency to tell lies in no way indicated a tendency to cheat in exams or commit fraud in later life.

Dr. Kang Lee, director of the Institute of Child Study at Toronto University, examined children aged 2–17. According to him parents should not be alarmed if their child tells a fib, they are not going to turn out to be pathological liars.

Almost all children lie and it is seen as a sign that they have reached a new developmental milestone. Those who have a more developed sense of reasoning lie better because they can cover up their tracks. Surprisingly, it has been discovered that children's aptitude for fibbing was not influenced by strict parenting or a religious upbringing.

Dr. Lee enticed children to lie by telling them not to peek at a purple Barney toy dinosaur placed behind their back. He then left the room for one minute – giving them ample time to look, while their reaction was filmed. Nine out of ten did turn round. But when asked by the tester, the majority denied it. While the study found the most deceitful age was 12, the propensity to fib dropped to about 70% once the children had turned 16.

✓ ***"Everyone is born sincere and die deceivers" - Marquis De Vauvenargues***

Scientists say it is very difficult to tell if your little one is lying after the age of eight, when they become better at disguising their deceit, this is known as the "Pinocchio peak". There are, however, one or two indicators – their facial expressions may be tense, there are inconsistencies in their story and they usually sound less spontaneous.

✓ ***"Pretty much all the honest truth telling in the world is done by children" - Oliver Wendell***

LIE DETECTORS

As far back as 1,000BC people have been trying to detect liars. The Chinese would force suspected liars to chew rice powder and then spit it out. If the power was dry, indicating a dry mouth, the suspect was thought to be lying.

In ancient Russia, the suspect would be forced to remove a ring from boiling water and if, three days later, there was no injury then they were declared innocent.

In this modern day and age there are even companies advertising home lie detector testing kits on the internet

Dr Paul Ekman, a psychologist and an undergraduate of the University of Chicago and New York, has pioneered the study of emotions and their connection to facial expressions and how they can be used in lie detection. Out of 20,000 people from all walks of life he found that only 50 people could spot deception without the help of formal training. Ekman also studied the rest of the body for signs of lying and said that when interviewed about the Monica Lewinsky scandal he could detect that former President Bill Clinton was lying because he used distancing language.

Dr Ekman has also worked with Computer Vision researcher, Professor Dimitris Metaxas, on designing a visual lie detector.

✓ ***"Whoever undertakes to set himself up as judge in the field of truth and knowledge is shipwrecked by the laughter of the Gods" - Albert Einstein***

The Mouth of Truth (Bocca della Verita)

The sculpture of a man-like face carved from Pavonazzetto marble is located in the portico of the church of Santa Maria in Cosmedin in Rome. Thought to be part of a first century Roman fountain it is most famous as its role as a lie detector.

Back in the Middle Ages it was believe that if someone told a lie with their hand in the mouth of the sculpture it would be bitten off! The Mouth of Truth featured in a memorable scene in the 1953 film "Roman Holiday" starring Gregory Peck and Audrey Hepburn as in the film neither of the two main characters are being truthful with each other.

The Polygraph or "Lie Detector"

These machines measure the physiological stress of a subject who has submitted to the test whilst answering a series of questions. They do not, as their nickname suggests, detect lies. The resulting spikes which show up on a graph are supposed to indicate lying. The accuracy of these machines is widely disputed and, in several well-known cases, has proved to be inaccurate. The use of the polygraph is far more established in the USA where it is claimed to have a 60-70% success rate. Its acceptance in the UK continues to increase but Mark Littlewood of Liberty commented that "We believe its widespread use would be a serious and unacceptable erosion of the right to silence."

✓ ***"When you want to fool the world, tell the truth"***
- Bismarck

However, in April 2007, the then Work and Pensions Secretary, John Hutton, stated that lie detectors would be used to help root out benefit cheats. The technology is already being used by the insurance industry in order to combat fraud.

In a recent survey Katie Maggs, Associate Medical Curator at the Science Museum, stated "Only a few people appear to accurately detect when someone is lying, but high-tech developers are working on creating more accurate technology.

Whether we will soon be using accurate lie detectors in the home or at work is hard to say, but it won't be long before this technology is readily available."

The survey showed almost a fifth of us believe lie detection is acceptable in everyday life, with more than one in ten saying it was OK in the workplace.

Back in 2005 a team at the University of Pennsylvania stated that monitoring the frontal lobe area of the brain shows when people are lying as apparently the frontal lobe is more active when people are lying.

In a functional magnetic resonance imaging scan (fMRI) volunteers were given two cards and asked to lie about one and tell the truth about the other. By analysing brain activity scientists were able to produce a formula that could detect lies from the truth which was 99% accurate.

Professor Ruben Gur, one of the team who worked on the study said "Now we can tell when the individual lies on a specific question.

✓ ***"Reality is bad enough, why should I tell the truth"? - Patrick Sky***

This is a major step forward. A lie is always more complicated than the truth, you think a bit more, and fMRI picks that up." However Dr Paul Seager, Senior Lecturer at the University of Central Lancashire in Social and Forensic Psychology is a psychologist who has focussed on how people behave when they lie said "You cannot generalise from lab studies to real life. Getting somebody to lie when there is really no consequence doesn't cut the mustard compared with a situation where the consequences could be being sent to prison."

He also added "nothing has so far been shown to be 99% effective in detecting liars."

Studies have shown that several factors, such as intuition, confidence and personality, come into play when detecting a lie.

A Professor Wiseman, who works at the University of Hertfordshire, told the BBC "People are really dreadful at detecting when someone is lying." They think that liars avoid eye contact and fidget a lot. In fact liars maintain more eye contact and they don't fidget". What you should look for apparently are long pauses between the questions asked and the answers given, the use of short sentences and lack of movement. Polygraph machines were also found to be poor at detecting lies as they detect when someone is stressed but not necessarily when they are lying.

✓ ***"Those who think it is permissible to tell white lies soon grow colour-blind" - Austin O'Malley***

Truth Drugs

It has been suggested that these have been proposed by the CIA in America who were said to want a universal "truth serum" but there is no evidence to support this claim. At the moment the unethical use of truth drugs is classified as a form of torture according to international law.

Medical thought would suggest that any information obtained through a truth drug can be unreliable. The subjects tend to mix fact with fiction as drugs increases talking.

✓ ***"A man may be an heretic in the truth, and if he believe things only because his pastor says so, or the assembly so determines, without knowing other reason, though his belief be true, yet the very truth he holds becomes his heresy" - F.W. Farrar***

PART TWO

LIES IN CHILDREN'S LITERATURE

Whilst not deliberately wanting to lie to children we often do so by using euphemisms. We tell children fairy stories, legends, and myths and also ask them to believe in Father Christmas, the Tooth Fairy and the Easter Bunny.

The world of literature has one or two notable stories for children about the results of lying. Who can forget Pinocchio? The fantasy story for children, by Carol Collodi, which featured a wooden puppet made from a piece of pine by a woodcarver named Geppetto who lived in a small Italian village. (The name Pinocchio is a Tuscan word meaning "pine-nut").

The wooden puppet eventually comes to life as a human boy (left, original art by Enrico Mazzanti). Pinocchio often got into trouble by his tendency to lie and his nose grew with every lie. The story was first published in Italy in 1883 and was translated into English in 1892. It has been a firm favourite with children ever since - they love the thought that Pinocchio's nose grows longer every time he tells a lie.

In 1940 the Walt Disney Corporation released a cartoon film, based on the story of Pinocchio and since then, long noses have become a caricature of liars.

✓ ***"The pure and simple truth is rarely pure and never simple" - Oscar Wilde***

Another example of the result of lying is told in one of the most famous of Aesop's fables, "The Boy Who Cried Wolf", also known as the Shepherd Boy and the Wolf. Aesop was a slave and a story teller who lived in ancient Greece between 620 and 560 BC. His fables, with their moral teaching, are amongst the best known in the world and remain a popular choice of children (right-Aesop, painted by Diego Velázquez).

The little boy in the story of "The Boy Who Cried Wolf" is a shepherd boy who gets so bored with looking after the sheep that he decides to entertain himself by calling out "wolf". Every time the nearby villagers came to his aid they found that the alarms were false and they had wasted their time. But, of course, the day came when the shepherd boy was actually confronted by a wolf but this time, when the boy cried help, the villagers did not believe his shouts for help and the flock perished. The moral of the story being of course the sentence at the end of the story "No one believes a liar – even when he tells the truth"

The Father Christmas Story

Almost everyone has grown up with the story of Father Christmas. Our parents told us about him from around the age of one. His existence was confirmed by family and friends, by books and movies. We wrote our Christmas lists to him which, on the whole, he managed to satisfy and on Christmas Eve we left him a drink and a mince pie which had always been half eaten by the morning.

✓ ***"Truth fears no questions" - Unknown***

We were in fact being duped by our family and society so why weren't we traumatised when we found out the truth? Was the lie more for the benefit of the adults rather than the children? Some people would say that it is unethical for parents to lie to their children and writer Austin Cline thinks that kids would find just as much enjoyment in knowing that their parents where responsible for buying their presents rather than some unknown stranger. However, Dr John Condry of Cornell University interviewed more than 500 children and found that not one child was angry with their parents for telling them about Father Christmas. He said that in actual fact the most common response to finding out the truth was that the children felt older and more mature, they knew they had been let in on a secret which the younger children didn't know.

On the subject of Father Christmas there was a wonderful article published in the New York Sun called "Yes, Virginia there is a Santa Clause", the details of which are as follows:

In 1897 an American, Dr. Philip O'Hanlon, a coroner's assistant on Manhattan's Upper West Side, was asked by his then eight-year-old daughter, Virginia, whether Santa Claus really existed.

Dr O'Hanlon suggested she write to the New York Sun, which was a prominent New York City newspaper at the time, assuring her that "If you see it in The Sun, then it is so."

✓ ***"Truth is beautiful, without doubt; but so are lies" - Ralph Waldo Emerson***

When one of the paper's editors, Francis Church, (pictured below) read the letter he decided to publish her letter and his reply in the paper. The reply from the veteran newsman has since become history's most reprinted newspaper editorial and Virginia's letter and Francis Church's reply are printed below:

"Dear Editor,
I am 8 years old. Some of my little friends say there is no Santa Claus. Papa says, 'If you see it in "The Sun" it's so.' Please tell me the truth; is there a Santa Claus?"

To: Virginia O'Hanlon
115 West Ninety-Fifth Street

"Virginia, your little friends are wrong. They have been affected by the scepticism of a sceptical age. They do not believe except [what] they see. They think that nothing can be which is not comprehensible by their little minds. All minds, Virginia, whether they be men's or children's, are little. In this great universe of ours man is a mere insect, an ant, in his intellect, as compared with the boundless world about him, as measured by the intelligence capable of grasping the whole of truth and knowledge.

(above - Virginia O'Hanlon)

✓ ***"Respect for the truth is an acquired taste" - Mark Van Doren***

Yes, Virginia, there is a Santa Claus. He exists as certainly as love and generosity and devotion exist, and you know that they abound and give to your life its highest beauty and joy. Alas, how dreary would be the world if there were no Santa Claus. It would be as dreary as if there were no Virginias.

There would be no childlike faith then, no poetry, and no romance to make tolerable this existence. We should have no enjoyment, except in sense and sight. The eternal light with which childhood fills the world would be extinguished.

Not believe in Santa Claus! You might as well not believe in fairies! You might get your Papa to hire men to watch in all the chimneys on Christmas Eve to catch Santa Claus, but even if they did not see Santa Claus coming down, what would that prove?

Nobody sees Santa Claus, but that is no sign that there is no Santa Claus. The most real things in the world are those that neither children nor men can see. Did you ever see fairies dancing on the lawn? Of course not, but that's no proof that they are not there. Nobody can conceive or imagine all the wonders there are unseen and unseeable in the world. You may tear apart the baby's rattle and see what makes the noise inside, but there is a veil covering the unseen world which not the strongest man, nor even the united strength of all the strongest men that ever lived, could tear apart.

✓ ***"Any fool can tell the truth, but it requires a man of some sense to know how to lie well" - Samuel Butler***

Only faith, fancy, poetry, love, romance, can push aside that curtain and view and picture the supernal beauty and glory beyond. Is it all real? Ah, Virginia, in all this world there is nothing else real and abiding.

No Santa Claus! Thank God he lives, and he lives forever. A thousand years from now, Virginia, nay, ten times ten thousand years from now, he will continue to make glad the heart of childhood."

Footnote

The editor's reply struck a very responsive cord and moved many people who read it. **More than a century later it remains the most reprinted editorial ever to run in any newspaper in the English language.** In 1972, after seeing Virginia O'Hanlon's obituary in the New York Times, four friends formed a company called Elizabeth Press and published a children's book called "Yes Virginia" that illustrated the editorial and included a brief history of the main characters. The book was then taken up by Warner Brothers who made an Emmy award-winning television documentary based on the newspaper editorial.

Virginia gave the original letter to one of her granddaughters, who pasted it in a scrapbook. It was feared that the letter was destroyed in a house fire, but thirty years after the fire, it was discovered intact. The original copy of the letter appeared and was authenticated by an appraiser on the "Antiques Roadshow" at $50,000.

✓ ***"When I tell the truth, it is not for the sake of convincing those who do not know it, but for the sake of defending those that do." - William Blake***

FABLES, FAIRY TALES, FOLKLORE, LEGENDS, MYTHS, OLD WIVES TALES AND SUPERSTITIONS

Since the very beginning of civilization all the above have been used to tell stories in order to amuse, educate and often intimidate. The stories could be both fascinating and frightening. In a time when the general populace could neither read nor write it was a way of communicating. Everyone could understand a story and storytelling has existed in every culture.

Fables

A fable is a story which has been passed down through the generations and aims to teach a lesson by way of using animals that can talk and act like people. As mentioned previously, the most famous fables were written by Aesop and his collection of Aesop's Fables, which number more than 600, have been read and quoted the world over. Apart from the fable already mentioned "The Little Boy Who Cried Wolf" (the moral being, it always pays to tell the truth), Aesop also wrote "The Monkey and the Dolphin". This is the story of a monkey who is thrown into the sea and is rescued by a dolphin. When the dolphin nears the shore not far from Athens he asks the monkey if he is an Athenian, the monkey answers that he is and that he is from a very noble family.

✓ ***"We do not err because truth is difficult to see. It is visible at a glance. We err because this is more comfortable" - Alexander Solzhenitsyn***

The dolphin then asks is he knew the Piraeus, the famous harbour of Athens, the monkey, thinking that that was the name of a man and knowing he had to back up his previous lie, answers that he knows him very well. The dolphin, realizing that monkey has lied to him all along, drops him into the sea and the monkey drowns.

The moral of the story being that once a lie is told then another lie invariably follows in order to cover up the first lie and sooner or later the lies will be discovered.

Another prolific teller of fables was the French poet Jean de La Fontaine (pictured left) whose fables of the 17th century are amongst the most famous in the world, and have been compared favourably with Aesop. Because he wrote about industrious ants, brave lions and carefree grasshoppers they were easily understood and loved. His first book of fables was dedicated to the grandson of Louis XIV.

Fairy Tales

A fairy tale is a term used for a short story which differs from legends and folklore in as much as the stories are usually about fairies, goblins, elves, giants and gnomes and are intended for children. The history of the fairy tale is very difficult to trace as they are not based on any specific time or place but we know they have existed for thousands of years.

- ✓ ***"Tell your friend a lie. If he keeps it secret, then tell him the truth" – Traditional Proverb***

They are usually set in some undisclosed time, usually starting "Once upon a time" and always have a happy ending. The name, fairy tale, is also used when we talk about happiness, as in a "fairy tale romance" or a "fairy tale ending". It can also refer to a very far fetched story which we tend not to believe, saying "Oh, that's a real fairy tale".

Some of the most famous of all fairy stories were written by Hans Christian Anderson, (pictured right), the Danish writer who, in the 1830's wrote "The Little Mermaid", "Thumbelina" and "The Red Shoes". One of his most famous quotes was "Life itself is the most wonderful fairy tale".

Equally famous were the fairy stories written by Jacob and Wilhelm Grimm known as the Brothers Grimm in the early 1800's (pictured left). Born in Hesse, Germany - Jacob in 1785 and Wilhelm in 1786 - they made a collection of fairy tales. They were both very interested in the folklore and legends of Germany and between 1816 and 1818 published two volumes of German Legends.

✓ ***"The history of our race, and each individual's experience, are sown thick with evidence that a truth is not hard to kill and that a lie told well is immortal." - Mark Twain***

Jakob in particular also started documenting the rules and relationship between similar words in different languages such as the English apple and the German apfel. The rules for such similarities became known as "Grimm's law".

Soon both brothers became the best known story tellers of folk tales in Europe and together published such tales as "Rumplestiltskin", "Snow White", "Cinderella", "Little Red Riding Hood" and "Hansel and Gretel".

One fairy all children like to believe in is, of course, the Tooth Fairy. This is the fairy that collects a baby tooth which a child has left under a pillow. Overnight the tooth is taken and replaced with money - much to their delight! It is even possible nowadays to send away for a Tooth Fairy letter and a Tooth Fairy dollar. The ritual of replacing lost baby teeth with money may have had its roots as far back as the time of the Vikings who had a "tooth fee" which was given to children when they lost a tooth. The teeth where then strung together to make a necklace which the Vikings warriors wore when they went into battle believing that this gave them power and luck.

Folklore

As with fables, folklore has been passed down from generation to generation and consists of oral history, music, proverbs, popular beliefs and even jokes.

✓ ***"There are only two ways of telling the complete truth - anonymously and posthumously" - Thomas Sowell***

Some folklore has a basis in truth but this has got lost in the mists of time along with the originators of such tales.

The word 'folklore' was first used in a letter in 1846 by the British writer, William Thoms, (picture right) and published by the London Journal "Athenaeum". Thoms invented the word to replace the terms, such as "popular antiquities" or "popular literature" which were used at the time. He was a great admirer of the work of Jacob Grimm, of the Grimm brothers.

Legends

Although legends may not be completely accurate they are in fact based on actual people. Their deeds or actions may have been exaggerated somewhat in order to teach a lesson or make the historical event more interesting. They usually tell of heroic characters and deeds. One famous English legend is, of course, King Arthur and, although there is quite a lot of controversy as to whether such a King existed, the point of the story was to show how such a King and his knights would have defended and helped their people.

✓ ***"It is easier to believe a lie that one has heard a thousand times than to believe a fact that no one has heard before" - Unknown***

Another such legend of a person defending and helping people is Robin Hood (pictured left with Maid Marian). There was a character called Robin of Loxley who lived in Nottinghamshire around the time of the Robin Hood story and he did help the poor but whether he lived in the forest with a band of men is debateable. Here again, for a legend to have survived, it was important that is was based on defending and helping people. Today the word "legend" has been somewhat corrupted and can apply equally to a footballer or film star whom the younger generation look up to and would like to emulate.

Magic

Reputable magicians will always admit that it is unethical to claim that their performance is anything but skillful deception. Jamy Ian Swiss, (pictured right) the American close-up magician who works mostly with cards, bills himself as an "honest liar". There are, however, others who are not quite so honest and use magic tricks for personal gain and will often use their skills to make people believe they have contacted ghosts or spirits. Con men for example will still use card tricks such as "Find the Lady" and the shell game, and although these are well known frauds, people still lose money on them.

✓ ***"A lie stands on one leg, the truth on two" – Benjamin Franklin***

In Los Angeles a shell-game ring was broken up as recently as 2009 when 10 people were arrested for victimizing dozens of downtown shoppers.

Myths

The Collins English Dictionary states that a myth is “a story about superhuman beings of an earlier age, from the Greek muthos meaning fable or word”. Myths are traditional stories which have been handed down from generation to generation, usually about spectacular events and how the natural world works. In very early times it was a way of explaining the science behind such events. Although no myths are real, some may once have been based on actual events and real people.

All the above, folklore, legends and myths, are very often hard to separate as all are tales which have been handed down through the years and very often overlap.

Superstitions

The Collins English Dictionary describes superstitions as “irrational belief usually founded on ignorance or fear and characterized by obsessive reverence for omens, charms, etc.” Superstitions are almost always based on luck, whether it is good or bad and, although quite irrational, very few of us would be without our own superstitions.

Who has not been wary about walking under a ladder or opening an umbrella indoors, and who has not said such things as “touch wood” or, on the first day of the month, “white rabbits”.

✓ ***“A little inaccuracy sometimes saves tons of explanation” - Saki***

Sports men and women seem particularly prone to superstition and will often have a certain ritual for getting ready for a big event.

Old Wives' Tales

"A foolish story, such as is told by garrulous old women" is how the Oxford dictionary defines an old wives' tale. They are a type of urban legend, almost like a proverb, and they are part of our oral tradition and as old as language itself.

In the first century, the apostle Paul wrote "But refuse profane and old wives' fables, and exercise thyself rather unto godliness" (I Timothy 4:7). The tales cover every subject under the sun from pregnancy, health, nutrition and wealth. Some tales, especially those dealing with health and sickness, are often based on fact. How many times have we heard about modern medicines which contain the basis of some old wives' remedy?

Urban legends

Whilst all the above have had a basis in the mists of time, urban legends are apocryphal stories which are very much a modern phenomenon dating back only as far as 1968. They are, in fact, a form of contemporary legend. These are tales based on something which happened to "a friend of a friend" and are spread like wildfire through the internet and e-mails and the abbreviation FOAF (friend of a friend) is now commonly used when referring to such stories.

✓ ***"It matters enormously if I alienate anyone from the truth" – C S Lewis***

Although not necessarily untrue, the urban legend is usually very exaggerated or distorted and the origin of the tale is usually impossible to trace as they famously do not contain specific dates, locations or names.

✓ ***"When a well-packaged web of lies has been sold gradually to the masses over generations, the truth will seem utterly preposterous and its speaker a raving lunatic" - Dresden James***

FAMOUS LIES

Anna Anderson, alias Anastasia

During the Russian revolution in 1918 the Bolsheviks massacred the Russian royal family. To ensure that no heir would survive to claim the royal throne they killed Tsar Nicholas II, his wife, son and four daughters. However, in 1920 someone came forward claiming that she was Princess Anastasia, the youngest daughter of the royal family, and that she had survived the massacre – her name was Anna Anderson.

(Ann Anderson left, Anastasia right).

With her resemblance to, and her boundless knowledge of, the Romanoffs, the Russian royal family, her claims were quite believable.

Controversy swirled around her but she ultimately lost her case in the legal proceedings that went on for years, she, however, stuck to her story until she died in 1984.

Many years later DNA tests were carried out on what proved to be the remains of the Romanoffs and Anna Anderson's claims proved to be false – she was not Princess Anastasia. It was only in 2009 that experts were able to confirm that all the remains of Czar Nicholas and his family had been found and that no one had escaped the massacre of 1918.

✓ ***"A lie has speed, but truth has endurance" - Edgar J. Mohn***

As Blind As A Bat

Wrong! A bat is not blind. Of all the 1,100 odd species of bats in the world not one of them is sightless and many of them can see very well indeed. The notion that a bat is blind probably arose because of the way they dart around at night catching insects which humans cannot see in the dark. A single bat can eat enough mosquitoes in a single evening to save several people from malaria and yellow fever. Laboratory tests have also shown that bats can distinguish shapes and colours.

The Dog with the Brandy

There is a popular misconception that St. Bernard dogs carry small kegs of brandy around their necks when rescuing victims from the snow. The dogs were initially bred by monks high in the Swiss Alps at the Hospice of St Bernard to help them rescue pilgrims trapped in the snow on their way from France to Italy. They have never carried the small kegs of brandy so often depicted. This was purely in the imagination of the English painter Edwin Landseer in the 1800's when he painted "Alpine Mastiffs Re-animating a Distressed Traveller".

✓ ***"Gradually I came to realize that people will more readily swallow lies than truth, as if the taste of lies was homey, appetizing: a habit" - Martha Gellhorn***

The dog in the painting wore a small barrel around its neck, supposedly full of brandy to revive the victim, which appealed to the public. This idea of giving brandy to someone trapped in the snow would have been the worst possible thing to do as alcohol would cause the outer blood vessels to dilate, blood would rush to the skin and the body temperature would decrease.

The St Bernard, which was last used in search and rescue operations in 1975, has now mostly been replaced by Golden Retrievers and German shepherd dogs.

Iago in Othello

William Shakespeare loved writing about deceit. "King Lear" is dominated by betrayal and lies, Brutus in "Julius Caesar" is a cold-blooded liar, but one of Shakespeare's most sinister characters, and one of his biggest liars, was Iago in the play "Othello".

The way he portrays Iago and his calculated deceit of Othello shows pure evil. Whilst Othello is honest and trustworthy his flag bearer Iago, although maintaining an outward air of honesty and dedication, is duplicitous and betrays Othello (above - Edwin Booth as Iago, c.1870).

✓ ***"The continued utterance of a lie does not make it true, but it does convince many that it is, particularly if you can squelch most efforts to expose the lie." Shapley R. Hunter***

He has a Machiavellian personality and hates Othello for passing him up for promotion and devises a plan to destroy the Moor. He works his deception so cleverly that other characters believe him to be a person most likely to be truthful.

As Othello's so called friend he tells lies about Othello's devoted wife, Desdemona, until, in a fit of jealousy, Othello kills her. When he realizes he has been deceived by Iago's lies, he kills himself.

Marie Antoinette

It is a lie to say that Marie Antoinette, (pictured right), the Queen consort of Louis XVI, ever said "let them eat cake" the phrase so associated with her.

One explanation is that it was the Spanish princess Marie Theresa, who was married to Louis XIV, who uttered the words 100 years earlier and the literal translation was "let them eat brioche". It refers to the fact that, at the time, French law required bakers to sell fancy brioche at the same price as ordinary bread, to prevent them selling only expensive bread, thus ensuring the peasants could afford to eat.

✓ ***"Materialism coarsens and petrifies everything, making everything vulgar, and every truth false" - Henri Frederic Amiel***

Another explanation is that the sentence was fictitious and was written in an autobiography by Jean-Jacques Rousseau published in 1769 who wanted to attack those in authority and thus help sell his book.

Paper Money – It's Not Made From Paper!

Paper money is, in fact, made from cotton or linen as these materials contain far fewer acids than wood pulp. This means they don't discolour or wear out so easily. In 1988 Australia became the first country to make bank notes from plastic which makes it much easier to incorporate security codes and holograms.

Potemkin Villages

The phrase "Potemkin villages" is an idiom based on an historical myth. Potemkin was the great love of Empress Catherine II of Russia and he supposedly built fake settlements to fool Catherine during her visit to the Crimea in 1787. He is supposed to have had facades of villages constructed in order to enhance his standing in the Empress's eyes.

Also, according to legend, the local governor of Tula, which is situated 120 miles south of Moscow, attempted a similar deception in 1787 when Catherine passed through on her way back from the trip in order to hide the effects of a bad harvest. The phrase "Potemkin village" has now come to mean, especially in a political context, anything meant to hide any potentially damaging situation.

✓ ***"If you want some lies to be believed wrap them up in truth" - Danish Proverb***

Pretender to the Throne

Born in 1475, Lambert Simnel was coached by Richard Simon (or Symonds) at the age of about ten to impersonate Richard, Duke of York, the younger son of Edward IV and so become an imposter and pretender to the English throne. However Simon later took Simnel to Ireland and claimed he was Edward, Earl of Warwick, also a claimant to the throne. From Ireland they gathered a number of supporters together and in 1487 crossed to England only to be defeated by Henry VII at the Battle of Stoke in 1487. Simnel was taken prisoner but, as a sign of Henry's lenience, was pardoned and later allowed to work for him.

Legend has it that the Yorkist pretender to the throne also invented the Simnel cake which we like to tuck into at Easter. Unfortunately this is just a nice rumour as the cake made with fruit and marzipan was being enjoyed long before Lambert Simnel was heard of.

Viscount Horatio Nelson

Admiral Viscount Horatio Nelson is one of the most remembered heroes of our history. Born into a fairly prosperous family in Norfolk he became an international hero in his own lifetime. Famous for his service in the Royal Navy, particularly during the Napoleonic Wars, he won several victories, including the Battle of Trafalgar in 1805, during which he was killed. Numerous monuments, including Nelson's Column in Trafalgar Square, London, have been created in his memory and his legacy remains highly influential BUT did you know that in fact Nelson never wore an eye patch?

✓ ***"An error does not become truth by reason of multiplied propagation, nor does truth become error because nobody sees it" - Gandhi***

He added an eye shade to his Admiral's hat, like a peak and he did not say "I see no ships." Instead, during the Battle of Copenhagen, in 1801, he said "I have only one eye. I have a right to be blind sometimes" and, raising his telescope to his blind eye he actually said "I really do not see the signal." (Nelson pictured right)

William the Conqueror

Contrary to popular belief William the Conqueror did not become King of England after the Battle of Hastings as he did not conquer straight away.

When Harold was killed at Hasting in October 1066 it was, in fact, Edgar the Aetheling, grand-nephew of Edward the Confessor, who was proclaimed king. The Anglo-Saxons did not rely on the hereditary system but elected their kings instead. Edgar reigned for just 2 months, but was never crowned, before escaping from William's invasion force.

✓ ***"I became a virtuoso of deceit. It wasn't pleasure I was after, it was knowledge. I consulted the strictest moralists to learn how to appear, philosophers to find out what to think and novelists to see what I could get away with. I distilled everything down to one wonderfully simple principle: win or die" – C Hampton***

HOAXES

It is believed that when the Protestant Reformation began in 1517 there was an attempt to reform the Catholic Church and scholars began to question whether texts and manuscripts were actually authentic or just a hoax. It is believed that Protestant jesters of the time began to ridicule the Latin phrase used in the Mass "Hoc est corpus meum" (for this is my body) and began calling it "hocus-pocus" which later became the word "hoax".

A hoax is the deliberate intention to deceive the public and gain their attention, there can be no such thing as a private hoax. The whole intention of a hoax is to gain notoriety. Quite often newspapers knowingly print a fake story which can be amusing, as in the case of an April Fool's hoax, but there is also misleading publicity, as in the case of false bomb threats, which are a hoax.

It wasn't until The Penny Papers of the 1830's developed the hoax that it became quite so popular and famous, to such an extent that the papers gradually developed the sensational headlines which we now associate with the tabloid newspapers of today.

One of the originators of the Penny Press was Benjamin Henry Day, the founder of the "New York Sun" which was the very first popular penny paper.

✓ ***"Truth resides in every human heart, and one has to search for it there, and to be guided by truth as one sees it. But no one has a right to coerce others to act according to his own view of truth" - Gandhi***

Day was also the inventor of the Ben-Day Dots printing process. It is said that it was he who stretched the truth to such an extent that it became known as sensationalism. "The New York Sun" was credited with writing the following story about life on the moon which, although it was fictional, was received by the public as fact in the summer of 1835.

Life on the Moon

"The New York Sun" announced during the last week of August 1835 that there was life on the moon. They stated that this discovery was the work of the famous British astronomer Sir John Herschel (pictured right). It described the moon as having large forests, inland seas and herds of bison wondering about. There was even evidence of intelligent life in the form of winged humans or "man bats" living there.

The newspaper sold in vast numbers, which was the purpose of the exercise but the whole thing was a complete hoax and Herschel was quite unaware of what was being claimed in his name. The author of the hoax was always believed to have been Richard Adams Locke, a reporter who worked for the paper, but he never ever admitted to this.

✓ ***"The least initial deviation from the truth is multiplied later a thousand fold" – Aristotle***

With his story about life on the moon, Locke went down in journalistic history as having published the greatest hoax of all time. The newspaper later published an article in which it discussed the story in great detail but, like Richard Adams Locke, it never admitted that the story was a hoax.

Ailments Cured by Electrons

Albert Abrams was born in America in 1863 and claimed to have invented machines which could both diagnose and cure almost any ailment by electrons. The system was known as ERA for Electronic Reactions of Abrams. The public was told that Abrams could diagnose any known illness from a drop of blood which could be sent through the post on a slip of paper.

In 1923 one of the ERA practitioners wrongly stated that he had completely cured a man who had been diagnosed with stomach cancer by the use of a machine called a Dynomizer. There was a public outcry when the man died a month later.

The American Medical Association tested one of Abrams practitioners with a blood sample and the result came back that the patient had been diagnosed with malaria, diabetes, cancer and syphilis. The blood sample had in fact come from a chicken! Similar tests were set for other practitioners who, as a result, found themselves facing fraud charges.

When Abrams died in 1924 the AMA examined one of the machines and found it contained nothing more than wires connected to buzzers and lights.

✓ ***"Integrity is telling myself the truth, and honesty is telling the truth to other people" - Spencer Johnson***

The Donside Contest

For many years the Donside Paper Company based in Aberdeen had sponsored a contest for graphic design students. In 2000 they asked the entrants to respond to one of three challenges: 1) to promote the Bermuda Triangle as a holiday destination, 2) to design a welcome pack for a shopaholics' association, or 3) to tell a lie convincingly. Many entries had already been received when the participating colleges received a letter from Donside saying that the contest regrettably had to be cancelled. The colleges duly began turning away new entries until they received a panic call from Donside asking them what they were doing. It was only then that the colleges realized that the cancellation letter had, in fact, been an entry from a contestant who had taken the third option and chosen to "tell a lie convincingly."

The colleges quickly tried to rectify the situation but were delayed by a fax from Donside announcing that the closing date had now been put back a month and that all entries would have to be re-submitted. As the colleges began to contact all the contestants they suddenly realized that they had been tricked again. Donside saw the funny side of the situation and announced that it was willing to judge the entry alongside all the others and made good it's promise when two students from the Edinburgh College of Art came forward and admitted being responsible for the rogue entry. Bill Gore, the Chief Executive of Donside personally awarded the prize in recognition of their creativity saying "It's the ultimate lie."

✓ ***"A single lie destroys a whole reputation for integrity" - Baltasar Gracian***

Phineas Taylor Barnum
One of the most famous hoaxers of all time was the famous American showman P T Barnum (pictured below). Born in 1810 he became famous for promoting hoaxes, calling himself the "Prince of Humbugs".

There is a very fine line between fraud and humbug, which by today's standards Barnum may have overstepped, but his customers at the time seemed to have enjoyed his shows so much that they overlooked this. Some of his most famous "acts" were:

Joice Heth, the 161 year old slave and nanny to George Washington;

The Fejee Mermaid which had a fish's body and the head of a baboon; and

A working model of Niagara Falls. Barnum had people rushing to his museum when he advertised this model – unfortunately for them the much advertised model turned out to be just 18 inches high!

Many have declared that Barnum's **Cardiff Giant** to be the greatest hoax of all time. Barnum got this idea from a George Hull who said he had "found" the 10 ft. giant on his land in New York in 1869 which he said must be from the race of giants in the Bible.

✓ ***"Not being known doesn't stop the truth from being true" - Richard Bach***

When Hull refused to sell Barnum the giant, Barnum decided to "find" one of his own. Hull filed a lawsuit against Barnum but the judge refused to hear the case unless Hull could prove that his "find" was genuine. The charges were subsequently dropped.

Berners Street Hoax

On 27 November, 1810 Theodore Hook (pictured below), a writer of comic operas, made a bet of one guinea with his friend Samuel Beazley that within a week he could make any house in London into one of the most talked about houses in the City.

He set about this by sending out hundreds of letters asking for a vast array of deliveries, assistance and visitors to an address in Berners Street. Chaos ensued as chimney sweeps, fleets of coal carts, vans delivering huge wedding cakes, fishmongers, shoemakers, doctors, vicars, lawyers and a dozen pianos began to block the street. Dignitaries such as The Duke of York, the Lord Mayor of the City of London, the Governor of the Bank of England and the Archbishop of Canterbury arrived. As the day continued the narrow street became completely congested bringing that part of London to a complete standstill. Although eventually confessing to the hoax, Hook was never punished.

✓ ***"Subtlety may deceive you; integrity never will" – Oliver Cromwell***

Betjeman Letter Hoax

Sir John Betjeman, who died in 1984, was a much loved poet, writer and broadcaster who had been a founder member of the Victorian Society and a great defender of its architecture.

When A N Wilson, one of London's most literary figures, published his biography of Sir John in August 2006 he became the victim of a hoax when he included in the book a letter giving details of a love affair which was supposed to have been written by Betjeman to a friend, Honor Tracy.

The letter had, however, been sent to Wilson by "Eve de Harben" (an anagram of Ever Been Had). It has always been believed that the letter had been written by Betjeman's authorised biographer and arch rival of A N Wilson, Bevis Hillier. Hillier has always denied all knowledge of the letter but did admit that it had just been too much when he had seen Wilson's book advertised as "the big one".

The Piltdown Man

This hoax which took place in 1912 concerned the finding, in Piltdown, East Sussex, of a skull and jawbone of a previously unknown early human. (pictured right).

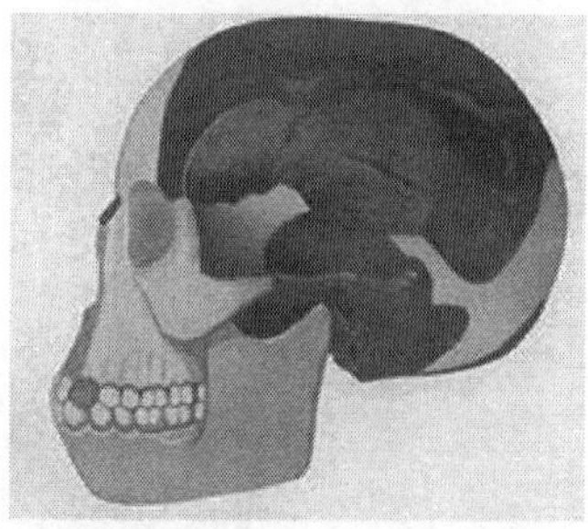

✓ ***"The history of the race, and each individual's experience, is thick with evidence that a truth is not hard to kill and that a lie told well is immortal" - Mark Twain***

This was the most famous paleontological hoax in history and the newspapers around the world ran headlines such as "Missing Link Found–Darwin's Theory Proved". Scientists at the time had been extremely anxious to find the missing link in the theory of evolution.

For more than 40 years many scientists believed the theory of the Piltdown Man and it wasn't until November 1953 that the news broke that the Piltdown Man had been a hoax and was in fact the jawbone of an orangutan and the skull of a modern human.

Although various people were suspected, amongst them even Sir Arthur Conan Doyle, no one has ever admitted being involved and it still remains one of the most intriguing hoaxes of all times.

The Book Which Didn't Exist

In the 1950's Jean Shepherd (pictured left), an American late night radio show host, played one of the biggest media hoaxes ever on his listeners.

He asked them to go into bookstores and ask for a copy of "I, Libertine", a book which didn't exist! With the title, author's name and a rough outline of the plot they went out in their droves.

✓ ***"All truths are easy to understand once they are discovered; the point is to discover them" - Galileo***

Bewildered by the sudden demand, booksellers started calling Publisher's Weekly trying to get their hands on copies. Articles appeared about the new book and the New York Times Book Review even included it in their list of newly published works and the Philadelphia Public Library actually opened up a card file.

Shepherd later wrote "It all started when I got into discussion one day about people who pretend to know everything." To illustrate the point he later said "Friends would call and tell me that they'd met people at cocktail parties who claimed to have read it." He had also been annoyed by the fact that best seller lists were compiled, not only from sales figures but also from requests for new books.

After a few weeks, the Wall Street Journal exposed the deception but the ultimate irony was that Ian Ballantine, a publisher who had been trying to get the paperback rights to the book, actually asked Shepherd to write the book. The fake book did in fact then become a real best seller and the proceeds donated to charity.

Jean Parker Shepherd died in 1999.

The Sawing off of Manhattan Island

This is a hoax about a hoax which never happened! In the 1800's New York had a Central Market where people gathered to discuss topics of the day.

✓ ***"It's not a matter of what is true that counts but a matter of what is perceived to be true" - Henry Kissinger***

One of the most respected orators was a retired ship carpenter called Lozier who began a rumour that Manhattan Island was, in fact, sinking because of the weight of urban development. Some of the audience expressed doubts about this but Lozier said he had proof and took them to the centre of the street and pointed to the fact that from City Hall to the other end was all downhill. As a result Lozier said that something must be done about the situation.

After a few days, he duly came back go to Central Market saying that he had found a solution to the problem which had been sanctioned by the Mayor – they would cut the island in two, tow it out and rotate it 180 degrees and then put it back together again so that Manhattan would be stabilized!

The story went that Lozier finally got together a huge workforce and the starting date was announced. Everyone involved was told to report at 6am for the groundbreaking ceremony when they would all march to City Hall. Thousands of people showed up – everyone it would seem with the exception of Lozier who was never seen again.

No newspaper reports of this fantastic story were ever found which led to the conclusion that the original story of the hoax was itself a hoax!

✓ ***"The men the American people admire most are the most daring liars. The men they most detest are those who try to tell them the truth" - Henry Louis***

The legendary plot was turned into a book called "New York Sawed in Half" by the American writer, Joel Rose, published by Bloomsbury in 2001. It reveals the complicity which exists between the hoaxer and the hoaxed. Vanity Fair described the book as "a suspenseful saga which relives the greatest hoax ever recorded in New York City history."

The Tasaday People

In August 1972 the National Geographic Magazine published a cover story about Manuel Elizalde Jnr, a wealthy Filipino politician, who had discovered a band of just 26 Stone Age people living deep in the rain forest in the Philippines, called the Tasaday. The National Geographic Society repeatedly showed a TV documentary on the group and a book, also based on the Tasadays, was published by American reporter John Nance. According to all reports the Tasadays were the most primitive people on earth using stone axes and living off the forest food.

Four months later Elizalde suddenly closed the base camp he had established to study the Tasaday and nothing more was heard of the group for the next 13 year when just as suddenly foreign journalists found the Tasadays living in houses and wearing western clothes.

Although it was later discovered that there was a small group of hunter-gatherers called Tasaday they certainly were not Stone Age people. They did lead separate lives but they traded with farmers living just a few miles away and the whole "discovery" had been a hoax.

✓ ***"Today I bent the truth to be kind, and I have no regrets, for I am far surer of what is kind than I am of what is true" - Robert Brault***

Russian Invasion is TV Hoax

On 14th March 2010 Georgians were informed by their TV station that Russia had invaded their country and that their President, Mikheil Saakashvili, had been murdered. Absolute panic broke out as Georgians crowded into the streets and families tried to reach each other.

Reporters from all over the world began trying to find out more but it was a senior reporter from the "Sunday Times" working in Georgia who sent the message which simply read "Not true".

Reminiscent of the H G Wells "War of the Worlds" hysteria a whole nation had been fooled. The hoax had in fact been planned by Saakashvili, who was alive and well.

Georgia's opposition party accused him of criminal recklessness and Kremlin politicians have pointed to the event to prove that Georgia's President was deranged. Later Saakashvili stated that a Russian attack remained "very realistic" and he was unapologetic.

Saakashvili took the independent station off the air and later handed it over to a government supporter and it now regularly shows pro-government opinion.

✓ ***"Honesty has a beautiful and refreshing simplicity about it. No ulterior motives, no hidden meanings. An absence of hypocrisy, duplicity, political games, and verbal superficiality. As honesty and real integrity characterize our lives, there will be no need to manipulate others" - Chuck Swindoll***

LITERARY HOAXES

There has been no lack of writers who have embellished stories such as misery memoirs and the holocaust memoirs, some of which may have had a grain of truth in them. However others, such as the following, have been complete hoaxes with the sheer intent of fooling the public for monetary gain.

Angel at the Fence

In 2008 a Holocaust memoir, entitled "Angel at the Fence" was exposed as a hoax just weeks before it was due to be published. Written by Herman Rosenblat, a 79 year old retired television repairman, the book relates how he met his future wife when, as a little girl, she tossed apples to him over the perimeter fence whilst he was being held in a concentration camp. Oprah Winfrey said of the book "it is the single greatest love story … we've ever told on air." Holocaust scholars doubted the story and it was reveled to be a hoax by "The New Republic" magazine in America.

Although Rosenblat was a Holocaust survivor the whole story was found to be false as other survivors insisted that civilians were not allowed anywhere near the fence which, in any case, was too high and the geography was all wrong. It was also discovered that Rosenblat's wife had lived more than 200 miles away from the camp.

✓ ***"Every time we fail to use words with care for their truthfulness, the honesty of everything we use words to express becomes progressively forsaken" – "New Yorker" Journalist***

Angry Penguins

The notorious Ernest Lalor "Ern" Malley was a completely fictitious poet and was at the heart of Australia's most famous literary hoax between 1943-44. The surname, Malley, is a pun on the word Mallee which is a class of native Australian vegetation and a bird, the Mallefowl.

The hoax was carried out by two writers, James McAuley and Harold Stewart in 1944 on the magazine "Angry Penguins" as they wanted to ridicule the pretentiousness of the journal and everyone connected with it, including its contributors. One afternoon they quickly wrote 16 poems which were supposed to be Ern Malley's tragic life's work. They lifted lines from books, from Shakespeare, a dictionary of quotations and even a report on the breeding grounds of mosquitoes! In fact they deliberately set out to produce what they thought was really bad verse.

According to the fictitious biography which accompanied the poems, Malley's work had only came to light after his death at the age of 25 when his sister, Ethel, found some unpublished poems among his things and sent them to the magazine "Angry Penguins". The editor was so impressed with them that he rushed out a special edition of the magazine which appeared in June 1945. The initial reaction was not what the editor had expected, with people suggesting that he had written them himself.

✓ ***"The opposite of a correct statement is a false statement but the opposite of a profound truth may well be another profound truth" -
Niels Bohr***

The following week the Sydney "Sunday Sun" ran a front page story naming McAuley and Stewart as the perpetrators of the hoax.

They, in turn, duly confessed to inventing Ern and Ethel Malley and also to writing the poems in an afternoon just putting down the first thing that came into their heads as a protest of "the loss of meaning and craftsmanship" in poetry.

For weeks afterwards the Ern Malley hoax featured on the front pages of the newspaper and many years later the editor claimed that he sympathised with the two writers' motivations.

Thomas Chatterton

Born near St Mary Redcliffe in 1752 Thomas Chatterton's father, a choirmaster, died just before Thomas was born and, as a result, Chatterton's childhood was relatively poor.

Although a poet in his own right it was his hoax of claiming to have found poems written by the 15th century monk Thomas Rowley, for which he is most remembered.

✓ ***"Men hate those to whom they have to lie" - Victor Hugo***

When the poems were "discovered" they were hailed as a wonderful find until, of course, the hoax was uncovered. Because of this Chatterton (pictured left) became notorious - he had even managed to convince Horace Walpole that the poems were genuine.

Chatterton died alone and in poverty at the age of 17 as a result of arsenic poising and never lived to see an edition of his poems published. There is some argument as to whether he committed suicide or whether he died as a result of self-medication to cure a venereal disease.

He was buried at the Shoe Lane Workhouse Cemetery in London. Unfortunately this cemetery no longer exists and no-one knows what happened to Chatterton's remains.

A statue of him was removed from St Mary Redcliffe's church, Bristol, when officials thought it was not suitable to have a monument to a suicidal boy on holy ground.

The Diary of Jack the Ripper

Controversy still surrounds the diary of Jack the Ripper which was published in 1993. It first came to light when a Michael Barrett, an unemployed scrap metal dealer, claimed that he had found it when he had been working on a house in Liverpool in 1992. Barrett claimed that it was the diary of a James Maybrick, (pictured overleaf) a Liverpool cotton trader, who claimed he had carried out the horrific Ripper murders in the East End in the 1880's.

✓ ***"As scarce as truth is, the supply has always been in excess of the demand" - Josh Billings***

If James Maybrick was in fact Jack the Ripper then his death in 1889 would explain why the murders ended when they did. Very few people, however, really believed it to be the genuine article and most dismissed it as a hoax.

In 1995 Barrett changed his story and swore in two separate affidavits that he was himself the author of the diary. The matter got even more confused though when his solicitor repudiated the affidavits and Barrett then withdrew the repudiation!

Fragments: Memories of a Wartime Childhood

First published in 1995 this autobiography by Binjamin Wilkomirski recounts his “fractured memories” as a Jewish boy caught up in the Holocaust. The narrative was in a fractured view of an overwhelmed Jewish boy. As a clarinettist and an instrument maker, Wilkomirski was living in Switzerland at the time and told of being held in two concentration camps before being sent to an orphanage in Krakow.

In 1999 Wilkomirski’s literary agent commissioned a Swiss historian to investigate various accusations which had been received. The historian duly reported his findings and it was found that the autobiography contradicted historical facts.

✓ ***“When in doubt, tell the truth” - Mark Twain***

In the controversy which followed, critics were quick to point out that "inventing" the Holocaust is just as harmful as "denying" it. As a "New Yorker" journalist wrote "Every time we fail to use words with care for their truthfulness, the honesty of everything we use words to express becomes progressively forsaken".

The Hitler Diaries

In 1983 extracts of what were purported to be Hitler's diaries were published in the West German news magazine "Stern". "The Sunday Times", in the belief that they were genuine, also devoted several pages to the story of the discovery in April of that year.

Supposedly recovered from an aircraft crash in 1945 they were found to be fakes shortly after publication. They had, apparently, been written by a well known German forger, Konrad Paul Kujau, using modern ink and paper and peppered with inaccuracies.

Kujau was born in Germany in 1938 and became a petty criminal and served two short jail sentences for theft. In 1970 he began illegally importing Nazi memorabilia and increased their value by forging documents to give them fake provenance. He also forged paintings purporting to be by Adolf Hitler. He soon realized there was a fortune to be made from such sales and in 1978 he sold his first "Hitler Diary" to a collector. Over the next two years a further 61 volumes were faked making Kujau a very rich man.

✓ ***"Please don't lie to me, unless you're absolutely sure I'll never find out the truth" - Shleigh Brilliant***

When the documents were found to be fakes shortly after publication Kujau was sent for trial on forgery and embezzlement charges and was sentenced to 42 months in prison.

After his release Kujau became a small time celebrity appearing on TV. He stood for Mayor of Stuttgart in 1996 and even set up his own company selling "genuine Kujau fakes". He died of cancer in 2000.

The Howard Hughes "Autobiography"

It was well known that Howard Hughes (pictured below) hated any sort of publicity and, by 1958, had become a recluse. However, in the early 1970's the American writer, Clifford Irving, created a sensation when he contacted his publishers, McGraw-Hill, claiming that he had been in touch with Howard Hughes who had agreed to let him co-write his autobiography. The publishers duly asked Irving to their offices where the writer produced forged letters stating that Hughes wanted the biography written but also wanted to keep the whole project a secret for the time being.

✓ ***"All great truths begin as blasphemies" - George Bernard Shaw***

Late in 1971 Irving duly delivered the biography, including notes purporting to have been written by Hughes, and McGraw-Hill made plans to publish the book in 1972. However, early that year Howard Hughes denounced Irving and began legal proceedings.

Irving eventually confessed to the hoax and was indicted on fraud and found guilty and spent 17 months in prison. "Time" magazine dubbed him "Con Man of the Year."

Irving later published a book called "The Hoax" relating the earlier events and a film, also called "The Hoax", was released in 1977 starring Richard Gere.

In Love and Consequences: a Memoir of Hope and Survival

The supposed memoir of Margaret B. Jones, the author told of a childhood of poverty and drugs in Los Angeles and being fostered by a mixed race family. The truth came out when her sister read an interview with Jones in "The New York Times".

In fact the author had grown up in an affluent, white family and attended an exclusive private school – even her name was false, she was in fact Margaret Seltzer.

✓ ***"All truth passes through three stages. First, it is ridiculed. Second, it is violently opposed. Third, it is accepted as being self-evident" - Arthur Schopenhauer***

Misha: A Memoire of the Holocaust Years
Supposedly written by a Misha Defonseca this 1997 book tells the "real life story" of a Jewish girl wandering through Europe in search of her deported parents. At one point she even claims to have been sheltered by a pack of wolves.

In 2008 Defonseca admitted it was a fabrication and that in actual fact she was the daughter of two Catholic members of the Belgian Resistance and that her real name was Monique de Wael. She later admitted that although her parents had been taken by the Nazis the rest was untrue saying "the story was my reality, my way of surviving."

My Life At the New York Times
"The New York Times" suffered one of its largest setbacks in its 152 year history when in and around 2003 one of its staff reporters, Jayson Blair, was found to have committed journalistic fraud. He had apparently made up stories, concocted scenes, taken material from other newspapers and generally created an impression that he had been at the actual scene of his reporting when, in fact, he had not.

Blair, then aged 27, resigned from the newspaper and in 2004 published a book entitled "Burning Down My Master's House–My Life At the New York Times" which told of his drug problems and his bipolar disorder. During the investigation into Blair's work "The Times" found problems with at least 36 of the 73 articles and the newspaper actually published an e-mail address for readers to contact them should they know of any other fabrications in Blair's work. As a result of his fraud, two top newspaper executives resigned.

✓ ***"There is no such thing as a harmless truth" - Gregory Nunn***

Pulitzer Prize Forgery

Janet Cooke, born in 1954 was the American journalist who won a Pulitzer Prize for a story she had fabricated in The Washington Post in 1980. The article, entitled "Jimmy's World", was about an 8 year old heroin addict.

The story caused such a stir that the police were asked to find the boy, without success. Doubts began to arise about the story but Bob Woodward, the Assistant Managing Editor, who himself helped The Washington Post win a Pulitzer prize for his Watergate reporting, put the story forward for the Pulitzer Prize for Feature Writing which Cooke won. Shortly afterwards the Post admitted the story to be a fraud.

Cooke duly resigned and returned the Prize. In a statement Cooke said "The article was a serious misrepresentation which I deeply regret. I apologize to my newspaper, my profession and the Pulitzer board and all seekers of the truth."

The last time the public heard of Cooke was in 1996 when, working in a department store for $6 an hour, she gave an interview in which she said that she had a lifelong compulsion to lie as a result of her upbringing. Apparently her father kept such a tight hold on the family purse strings that the family had to buy things in secret. She added "The conclusion I've come to is that lying from a very early age was the best survival mechanism available."

✓ ***"Every violation of truth is not only a sort of suicide in the liar, but is a stab at the health of human society." - Ralph Waldo Emerson***

The Awful Disclosures of Maria Monk

This sensational autobiography tells the story of a Canadian woman, Maria Monk (fictionalised picture below), who had been sexually exploited in her convent. Entitled "Awful Disclosures of Maria Monk, or The Hidden Secrets of a Nun's Life in a Convent Exposed" was published in 1836.

The book caused a public outcry with Protestants in Montreal wanting an investigation. Historians had already been convinced that the whole account was false and this proved to be so when the investigation found no evidence to support the claims. One newspaper editor, after interviewing Monk, concluded that she had never been in a convent.

In 1839 "The Boston Pilot" published her obituary stating that she had died in an almshouse.

Salamander Letter

The above forged letter was composed by a Mark Hoffman and led to one of the strangest incidents in the Mormon Church. Two murders occurred in Salt Lake City in 1985 in an attempted cover-up.

✓ ***"I believe that love of truth is the basis of all real virtue, and that virtues based upon lies can only do harm" - Bertrand Russell***

The leaders of the Latter Day Saints believed the letter, purported to have been written by early Mormon leaders, to be genuine when Hoffman said he had found them in an old Bible. The Church made the decision to buy the letter which was supposedly in Reformed Egyptian characters from the Golden Plates which the Latter Day Saints believe are the source of the sacred text of their faith from the Book of Mormon. According to their religion the Golden Plates were shown to Joseph by a white salamander.

The document was subsequently found to be a forgery and Hoffman resorted to killing in order to cover up his tracks. Hoffman, however, became the victim of the car bomb he had made himself when the bomb exploded in his car before reaching its intended target. It was this which gave the police the link they needed to connect him to earlier murders.

The Salamander Letter is now in the Mormon Church vaults.

The Shakespeare Forgeries

Although William Ireland, born in England in 1775, was a writer of gothic novels and a poet he will always be remembered as a forger of Shakespearean documents. William, who had been a great disappointment to his father, decided to gain his father's approval by presenting him with a deed which contained the signature of Shakespeare. His father, a collector of anything Shakespearian, was delighted with his gift and, of course, with his son.

✓ ***"Humility is nothing but truth, and pride is nothing but lying" - Vincent de Paul***

Unfortunately, Ireland did not stop there. He went on to "find" an assortment of Shakespeare's notes and manuscripts which he said he had discovered in a package of old documents belonging to a friend who wanted to remain anonymous. In 1795 he even "found" a whole new play by Shakespeare called "Vortigern and Rowena". The so called experts of the day authenticated all the documents.

Hearing of a newly found Shakespearean play, the playwright Richard Sheridan purchased the rights for its first production at the Drury Lane Theatre.

Two days before the play was due to open, Edmond Malone, an authority on Shakespeare's plays, released an attack on the authenticity of Ireland's discoveries. The play, however, opened to a packed house but ended with catcalls and closed after only one performance.

Ireland died a poor man in 1835.

Shattered Glass

Another American journalist, Stephen Glass, who became famous for his lies, was the 25 year old associate editor of the political magazine "The New Republic". In the 1990's Glass, who was the rising star of Washington journalism, not only managed to deceive his editor with fabricated stories over a 3 year period he even created fake sources and websites to cover his tracks.

✓ ***"There is no lie that a man will not believe; and there is no man who does not believe many lies; and there is no man who believes only lies" - John Sterling***

In the end, the editor of the magazine, Charles Lane, exposed Glass by saying that at least 27 of the 41 stories written by Glass were false. These included stories on the Center for Science in the Public Interest, the organization Drug Abuse Resistance Education, the Conservative Political Action Conference and Hofstra University.

Five years after his dismissal a feature film about the whole episode called "Shattered Glass" was released in 2003 starring Hayden Christensen with the tagline "He would do anything just to get a great story."

In 2003 Glass also published a novel called "The Fabulist" telling his story with a very similar line – "a novel of an ignominious fall, the rise to infamy, and life after both."

Glass was last known to be living in New York and hopes to be admitted to the bar.

✓ ***"It often happens that if a lie be believed, only for an hour, it has done its work and there is no further occasion for it" – Jonathan Swift***

APRIL FOOL HOAXES

The origin of April Fools' Day is lost in the mists of time but it is known that it is connected to the coming of Spring and the practical jokes date back to Roman times. The Celts and Ancient Romans actually celebrated with a festival of practical joking at the Vernal Equinox.

Now, of course, April Fools' Day hoaxes have taken on a life of their own and in fact have proved to be quite acceptable and really enjoyable. Unlike most other hoaxes, the general public would feel quite deprived if their newspaper didn't carry some sort of April Fools' Day hoax on the first of April each year.

The newspapers can get away with anything on this day – whether it is advertising a new bubble for a spirit level, a tube of elbow grease or a left handed Mars bar – as the American writer Mark Twain (pictured right) once said "This is the day upon which we are reminded of what we are on the other 364."

The success of The Guardian newspaper's April Fools' Day joke in 1977 about a small republic in the Indian Ocean, called San Serriffe (see page 79), is widely credited with making the annual joke such a success with the British tabloids over the following years.

✓ ***"Truth is the torch that gleams through the fog without dispelling it" - Claud-Adrian Helvetius***

Internet Shut Down for Spring Cleaning

In 1997 an e-mail, supposedly from the Massachusetts Institute of Technology, went round the internet reminding users that the internet would be closed down for 24 hours for its annual spring clean. Apparently this was necessary to clean out all the "electronic flotsam and jetsam" that had accumulated. Customers were told that "Five very powerful Japanese-built multi-lingual internet-crawling robots situated around the world will search the Internet and delete any data that they find".

This was apparently the Internet version of the old 'phone systems spring clean when customers were advised to place bags over the 'phone to catch any dust etc which might be blown out during the clean!

Guinness Mean Time

In 1998 Guinness Brewery issued a press release stating that, in an agreement with the Old Royal Observatory, they would be the official sponsor of the Observatory millennium celebration. As a result of this agreement Greenwich Mean Time would, until the end of 1999, be called Guinness Mean Time and the Observatory would change the name of seconds to "pint drips".

✓ ***"The folks who know the truth aren't talking. The ones who don't have a clue, you can't shut them up!" - Tom Waits***

Not realising that this was a joke, "The Financial Times" announced the news and wrote a very terse article to the effect that the excitement over the millennium was being exploited by some companies who were being seen as too eager to promote their own brands and declared that Guinness was setting a "brash tone for the millennium".

"The Financial Times" eventually realized its mistake and published a retraction stating the news "was apparently intended as part of an April 1st spoof."

The Left-Handed Whopper

It was in 1998 that a full page advertisement appeared in "USA Today" stating that Burger King was bringing out a new addition to their menu called "The Left Handed Whopper". This new burger had apparently been designed to meet the needs of the 32 million left-handed people in America. According to their advertisement Burger King's new Whopper would be made in exactly the same way as the original burger with lettuce, tomato and hamburger patty but, for the benefit of their left-handed customers, everything would be rotated by 180 degrees!

Burger King later released a follow up notice stating that thousands of customers had gone into their food outlets and ordered the new burger and many others had gone in saying that they did not want the new left-handed Whopper and would rather have their original right-handed version.

✓ ***"Many people today don't want honest answers insofar as honest means unpleasant or disturbing. They want a soft answer that turneth away anxiety" - Louis Kronenberger***

San Serriffe

As mentioned previously, in 1977 "The Guardian" newspaper published a supplement on San Serriffe, a small republic located in the Indian Ocean made up of two main semi-colon shaped islands called Upper Caisse and Lower Caisse which were run by a senior officer called General Pica. All day long hundreds of readers rang "The Guardian" asking for more information on what seemed like an ideal holiday destination. They even rang travel agents and tried to make bookings.

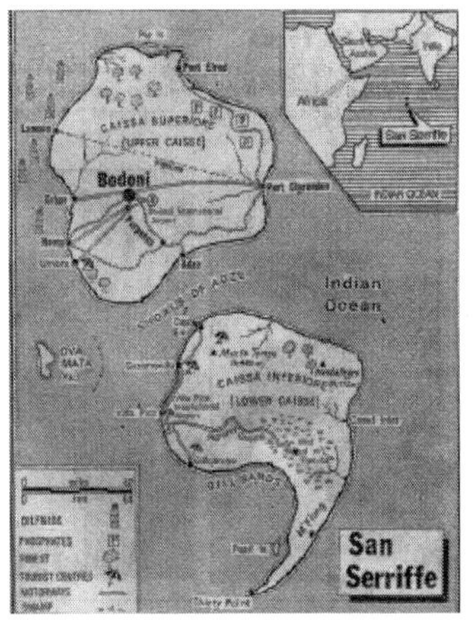

What no-one seemed to realize was that Serif is a term used in the printing industry, probably of Dutch origin, which is a fine line finishing. A font which uses it is called a Serif font and fonts which don't use it are called "Sans Serif". Whilst uppercase and lower case are capital letters and small letters.

Gradually it dawned on everyone that they had been taken in by an elaborate April Fools joke devised by Philip Davies, who was head of the Special Reports department at "The Guardian" and that everything about the islands was named after printer's terminology.

The success of the San Serriffe hoax is widely acknowledged as the inspiration for the April Fool's Day hoaxes which has gripped British tabloids ever since.

✓ ***"I was provided with additional input that was radically different from the truth. I assisted in furthering that version" - Oliver North***

Spaghetti Bush

In 1957 the BBC fooled an entire nation when Panorama broadcast a three minute hoax documentary about a bumper spaghetti harvest in southern Switzerland.

Narrated as it was by the BBC's top broadcaster, Richard Dimbleby, the usually very prim and proper Panorama programme showed a family carefully harvesting strands of spaghetti from a bush and laying the strands out to dry in the sun. It also explained how, thanks to the hard work of the growers, the strands always grew to the same length each year and how a severe frost could impair the flavour.

Some viewers criticised the hoax for being shown on a serious factual programme whilst others flooded the switchboard with calls wanting to know where they could purchase such a bush for themselves.

The Spaghetti bush was the idea of cameraman, Charles de Jaeger and was perhaps the very first time that television had been used in an April Fools' Day hoax. He was given permission to film the three minute slot in Switzerland.

In 1999 the Birmingham Post listed the hoax as No. 82 in TV's 100 greatest moments.

✓ ***"Whatever is only almost true is quite false, and among the most dangerous of errors, because being so near truth, it is the more likely to lead astray" –Henry Ward Beecher***

Taco Bell buys the Liberty Bell

Taco Bell, the American restaurant chain which specializes in Mexican-style food, announced on 1st April 1996 that it had bought the Liberty Bell, the iconic symbol of American Independence, and was going to rename it the Taco Liberty Bell. Their statement, in a full page advertisement in six major American newspapers, ran as follows:

"In an effort to help the national debt, Taco Bell is pleased to announce that we have agreed to purchase the Liberty Bell, one of our country's most historic treasures. It will now be called the "Taco Liberty Bell" and will still be accessible to the American public for viewing. While some may find this controversial, we hope our move will prompt other corporations to take similar action to do their part to reduce the country's debt".

Hundreds of angry citizens rang the National Historic Park in Philadelphia where the bell was housed to protest at such an act. At noon Taco Bell issued a second statement in which they confessed to the hoax, adding that they would also donate $50,000 for the upkeep of the Liberty Bell.

✓ ***"Without seeking, truth cannot be known at all. It can neither be declared from pulpits, nor set down in articles, nor in any wise prepared and sold in packages ready for use. Truth must be ground for every man by himself out of it's husk, with such help as he can get, indeed, but not without stern labour of his own" – John Ruskin***

CONFIDENCE TRICKSTERS

A Confidence Trickster, or con man, is a plausible character who is also a swindler. He makes his living by earning a victim's trust and then exploits their human qualities of greed and naïveté. The term con man was first used in the mid-19th century at the trail of con man William Thompson (see page 84).

The one common factor is that the victim, or "mark", entirely believes in the good faith of the con-artist. Unfortunately almost anyone can fall victim to the con-artist, they are only limited by their greed. Sometimes the victim will even try to con the con-artist only to discover that they have been manipulated from the very start. There is a saying among con men that "you can't cheat an honest man" but the French poet Jean de la Fontain summed it up quite differently when he said "It is twice the pleasure to deceive the deceiver".

Con men will often employ someone called "a shill" or an accomplice. It's "the shill's" job to pretend they know nothing about the con man and be an enthusiastic and independent customer. The exploits of con men have been the basis of many films and books such as "Catch Me If You Can" and "The Sting" (see pages 88 & 184), and it would be impossible to list all the confidence tricksters who have operated at one time or another but a few of the most famous scams and their operators are listed on the following pages.

✓ ***"I imagine a man must have a good deal of vanity who believes, and a good deal of boldness who affirms, that all the doctrines he holds, are true, and all he rejects are false." - Benjamin Franklin***

The Spanish Prisoner Trick

One of the oldest known confidence tricks in the world is known as "The Spanish Prison" which originated in England in the 16th century.

It was during the reign of Elizabeth I when England was under constant threat of invasion from Spain that the con became famous. It has, of course, many variations but basically a con man tells a wealthy "victim" about a wealthy man being imprisoned by King Philip II of Spain under a false identity. The real identity of the person cannot, of course, be revealed as strict secrecy is required but, if enough money can be raised for his release, the rewards will be great. After the victim has given over some money difficulties arise which require more money to be raised, then more and more. Finally the victim has given everything he has and then the con man disappears.

The Spanish Prisoner Trick has been the basis of all long term cons and has many modern variants.

Today we have such cons as the Advance Fee Fraud, the Overpayment Scam, and the Lottery E-Mail Scam. All want money up front to cover administration costs etc – i.e. paying money for a promise of wealth. Sometimes known as the 419 Fraud this con is largely carried out by e-mail which usually comes from Africa. As the fraud started in Nigeria the term 419 was used as it stems from that part of Nigerian law which deals with scams.

✓ ***"Most of the greatest evils that man has inflicted upon man have come through people feeling quite certain about something which, in fact, was false" - Bertrand Russell***

Trust Me With Your Watch

The term "con man" was first used in the 1850's at the trial of American criminal, William Thompson, who had the very simple technique of asking people if they had confidence in him. Dressing himself up to look a highly respected gentleman he would walk up to upper class people and, pretending to know them, would ask "Have you the confidence in me to trust me with your watch until tomorrow." Feeling that they should remember him, the victim felt duty bound to show their trust in him and so lend him their watch. After taking the watch Thompson would walk away never to return.

He was arrested and tried in 1849, the newspapers dubbing him "the confidence man" which was later shortened to con man.

Secret Service Most Wanted

Born in 1969, Matthew Bevan Cox (pictured right) is an American con man who falsified documents to make it look as though he owned properties and then, on the back of these documents, obtained several mortgages for five or six times their worth.

✓ ***"If a lie is repeated often enough all the dumb jackasses in the world not only get to believe it, they even swear by it" - Billy Boy Franklin***

Over a period of time it has been estimated that he acquired up to $25 million and his activities spread over the southern United States. As a result of these activities he was eventually put on the Secret Service's Most Wanted List.

Arrested in 2006 and indicted on 42 counts he faced a prison sentence of up to 400 years but plea bargained his sentence which was duly reduced to 54 years.

He is currently serving his sentence in a low security prison in Florida.

The 1872 Diamond Hoax

Two cousins, Philip Arnold and John Slack were the confidence tricksters behind the above legendary hoax. In 1871 the two prospectors travelled to San Francisco where they said they had found a diamond mine and produced a bag of diamonds as proof. A mining engineer was sent to examine the field and found diamonds, which he valued at approximately $150,000. Tiffany's persuaded the couple to sell their interest in the field for $660,000. Later it was discovered the Arnold and Slack had bought cheap cast-off diamonds from Europe for $35,000 and scattered them around the field.

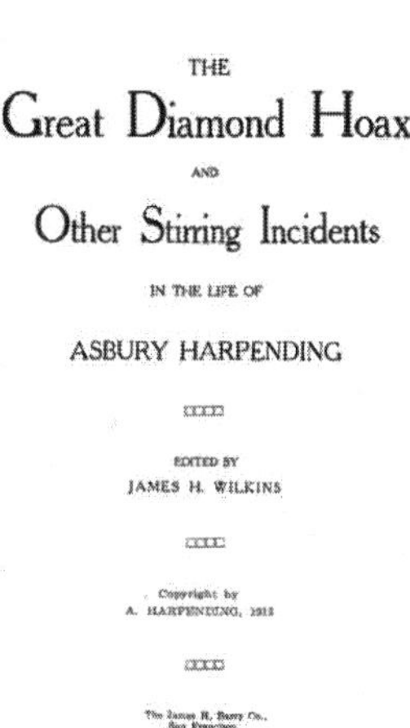

THE

Great Diamond Hoax

AND

Other Stirring Incidents

IN THE LIFE OF

ASBURY HARPENDING

EDITED BY

JAMES H. WILKINS

Copyright by

A. HARPENDING

(Above – book written by the mine promoter about the affair)

✓ ***"A lie may take care of the present, but it has no future" - Author Unknown***

Born in Kent in 1829, Arnold returned to his home town in Kentucky and became a successful banker but the diamond investors sued him and he settled for an undisclosed amount. Years later Arnold died from pneumonia after he had been wounded in a gun fight with a rival banker.

John Slack disappeared for a while and lived quietly in New Mexico 1896 and died at the age of 76.

In 1963 their story was told on the TV series "The Great Adventure". The episode was called "The Great Diamond Mountain".

Million Dollar Bunco Ring

The above ring, run by Lou Blonger, was an extensive ring of confidence tricksters that operated in Denver, Colorado for more than 25 years until they were brought to trial in 1923. Operating very much on the lines of "The Sting" Blonger's ring had rooms set up as betting shops from which to operate the big cons. Unsuspecting tourists were asked to put up large amounts of money in order to receive winning bets as in the wire con shown in "The Sting".

Lou Blonger had had the odd legal problem from some of the people he had defrauded but the organization went largely unchallenged until he was well into his 70s. As Blonger had connections with various Denver politicians and police officials, it was the District Attorney, Philip S Van Cise, who decided to bypass the police department and use his own force to arrest Bolger and 33 of his con men.

✓ ***"The search for truth implies a duty. One must not conceal any part of what one has recognized to be true" - Albert Einstein***

In a highly publicised trial the "Bunco King" and the rest of the gang were convicted and sent to prison and Lou Blonger died there in April, 1924 just six months after he arrived.

The Ritz Hotel Is Up For Sale

In 2006, two unemployed men, Anthony Lee and Patrick Dolan, managed to persuade Terry Collins, the co-founder of London Allied Holdings, that the Ritz Hotel in London, open since 1906 and noted for its opulence, was up for sale at the knock-down price of £250 million. Unbeknown to Collins the hotel, with an estimated market value of £600 million, was not for sale.

In December 2006 Collins handed over a deposit of £1,000,000 for the purchase of non-existent documentation supposedly in the hands of solicitors.

At the end of the trial in July 2010 Lee, from Goole in Yorkshire, was jailed for 5 years at Southwark Crown Court. Sentencing him for the 'elaborate and outrageous' sting Judge Stephen Robbins said "This offence has been compared with other fraudsters from the past, who tried to sell the Eiffel Tower, Brooklyn Bridge and Buckingham Palace."

Brooklyn Bridge for Sale

George Parker, one of the most audacious con men in American history, made a living selling New York landmarks.

✓ ***"It is always the best policy to tell the truth, unless, of course, you are an exceptionally good liar" – Jerome K. Jerome***

Although he sold many landmarks, such as Madison Square Garden, The Metropolitan Museum, the Statue of Liberty and Grant's Tomb during the early 1900's his favourite site was the Brooklyn Bridge which he sold twice a week for several years! From his fake "office" he produced impressive forged documents to prove his right of ownership.

After his third conviction for fraud in 1928 he was sentenced to life imprisonment in Sing Sing Prison where he spent the last 8 years of his life.

He is remembered as a very talented hoaxer and one of the most successful con men in the history of the United Sates.

Catch Me If You Can

One of the most famous of modern con men is Frank Abagnale, an American born in 1948, who became the subject of a film called "Catch Me If You Can". Whilst still a teenager, he became known as a confidence trickster, cheque forger, and skilled imposter. Abagnale managed to con his way through $2 million worth of cheques. He also pretended to be a doctor, a lawyer and a Pan Am pilot. He twice escaped from custody but was eventually caught in France in 1969 and was then extradited to Sweden.

At his trial for forgery the defence attorney argued that he had "created" cheques and not forged them.

✓ ***"In the matter of a difficult question it is more likely that the truth should have been discovered by the few than by the many" – Rene Descartes***

In 1974, after serving less than 5 years in prison, the United States federal government made a deal with him, the deal being that they would release him on condition that he helped them solve crimes committed by fraudsters and con men.

Abagnale is now a security consultant and lecturer for the FBI and runs his own financial fraud consultancy company!

The Enron Scandal

In 2001 the above corruption scandal broke when Kenneth Lee "Ken" Lay, the CEO and Chairman of the Enron Corporation since 1985 was charged with accounting fraud.

In less than 15 years Enron had become America's seventh largest company, operating in more than 40 countries and employing 21,000 staff.

But it all turned out to have been a fraud as Enron had lied about its profits, had concealed debts and had produced incorrect company accounts. As more facts were revealed investors retreated forcing the company into bankruptcy.

In July 2004 Lay was indicted by a grand jury on 11 counts of fraud and was found guilty in 2006 on 10 counts.

Also named were Andrew Fastow, former Chief Financial Officer, and the author of the false accounting and David Duncan, Enron's Chief Auditor who had shredded key documents.

✓ ***"Half a truth is often a great lie" - Benjamin Franklin***

Facing a possible 20-30 years in prison Lay died whilst on holiday in Colorado just three and a half months before his sentencing. Autopsy reports say that he died of a heart attack caused by coronary artery disease but there have been conspiracy theories surround his death.

Trafalgar Square for Sale

In 1923 a retired Glasgow born actor, Arthur Furguson, met a rich American in London and told him that the statue of Admiral Lord Nelson in Trafalgar Square had to be sold along with all the lions and fountains in the square to help pay for Britain's enormous debts. Apparently Britain was prepared to accept a cheque right away in order to complete the deal.

The American fell for the story and gave Furguson a cheque and whilst Ferguson went off to cash it the American tried to hire some contractors. They, of course, were very reluctant to believe the story and told him why, but it was not until the American received an official confirmation from Scotland Yard that he finally believed that he had been conned.

That summer the police also learned of another American who had paid £1,000 for Big Ben and another who had made a down payment of £2,000 for Buckingham Palace. All were believed to have been conned by Arthur Furguson.

✓ ***"Truth never damages a cause that is just" – Mahatma Gandhi***

Furguson emigrated to America in 1925 and, whilst in New York, found an Australian who was interested in buying the Statue of Liberty. Foolishly perhaps, Furguson agreed to have his photograph taken with the buyer in front of the Statue. Unfortunately there was a delay in raising the £100,000 deposit and the Australian became suspicious. He took the photograph to the police who immediately arrested Furguson.

He was jailed for 5 years and released in 1930 and lived in luxury and continued to defraud people until he died in 1938.

The Man Who Sold the Eiffel Tower – Twice!

In 1925 Victor Lustig, a con man, got together six scrap metal dealers and told them that the French government wished to sell off the tower as it was far too expensive to maintain. The Eiffel Tower, which had been built for the 1889 Paris Exposition, had been due to be demolished in 1909. Lustig duly "sold" the Tower to one of the dealers and made off to Vienna with all the cash.

Too embarrassed to complain, the scrap metal dealer did not report the incident to the police so Lustig was able to return to Paris and tried to sell the Tower once again!

✓ ***"All deception in the course of life is indeed nothing else but a lie reduced to practice, and falsehood passing from words into things" - Robert Southey***

This time the scam was reported but Lustig managed to evade arrest and later went into counterfeiting and was arrested in 1935.

At his trial Lustig pleaded guilty and was sent to Alcatraz for 20 years. In 1947, however, he contracted pneumonia and died two days later. On his death certificate his occupation was listed as "apprentice salesman!".

ZZZZ Best

The above company was owned by Barry Minkow, an American religious leader and ex-convict. Born in 1967, Minkow became a fraudulent entrepreneur whilst still in his teens.

His business, pronounced "Zee Best" seemed to be a thriving carpet cleaning business but it collapsed in 1987 costing investors over $100 million. The Los Angeles Times revealed that Minkow had run up $72,000 in fraudulent credit card charges.

Convicted of fraud for misappropriating $23 million of the company funds, Minkow was sentenced to 25 years but served only seven years. It was whilst he was in prison that he saw the error of his ways and became involved in religion.

Minkow is now a senior pastor in San Diego and is recognized as an expert on fraud, lecturing to universities and business communities in an effort to stop same.

- ✓ ***"If one is to be called a liar, one may as well make an effort to deserve the name" - A. A. Milne***

King Con

Steven Jay Russell is currently serving a 144 year jail sentence for being a long established con man who also made a series of amazing jail breaks.

Like the con man Frank Abagnale (see pages 180), by using at least 14 known aliases Russell forged credentials and passed himself off as a judge, a doctor, and an FBI Agent. He also earned himself the names "Houdini" and "King Con" for his remarkable ability to escape from jail.

Whilst in jail on minor insurance fraud charges, and having already escaped four times from several Texan jails, he met and fell in love with a fellow inmate, Phillip Morris. On his release, and in order to gain money to fund their lifestyle, Russell pulled off his scams.

He managed to get a job with a medical insurance company as their chief financial officer after showing them his forged CV. In five months he embezzled some $800,000.

When he was eventually found out and sentenced he impersonated a judge over the telephone and requested that his own bail money be lowered from $900,000 to $45,000, which he then paid with a cheque which later bounced.

The story of Steven Russell has been made into a film starring Jim Carey and Ewan McGregor (see page 180) entitled "I Love You Phillip Morris."

✓ ***"A deception that elevates us is dearer than a host of low truths" - Marina Tsvetaeva***

A Fake Rockefeller

Christopher Rocancourt was born in France in 1967 and his first big con was in Paris where he faked the deeds to a property which he did not own and "sold" it for almost a million pounds. He later made his way to New York and posed as a French member of the Rockefeller family and a venture capitalist.

In 2002 he pleaded guilty to charges of theft, grand larceny, smuggling, bribery, perjury and fraud against 19 victims and was fined $9 million and sentenced to 5 years in prison. He once estimated that his various scams had made him at least $40 million. In Switzerland the police have connected him with a jewel theft and barred him from the country until 2016.

Quiz Show Scandal

In the 1950's a quiz show in America came to prominence when a man called Charles van Doren, an assistant professor at Columbia University, began a winning streak on a TV quiz programme called "Twenty One" which earned him a small fortune and an appearance on the cover of "Time" magazine.

✓ ***"Ah yes, truth. Funny how everyone is always asking for it but when they get it they don't believe it because it's not the truth they want to hear" - Helena Cassadine***

When he was first accused of cheating he strongly denied it saying "It's silly and distressing to think that people don't have more faith in quiz shows." But in 1959 he confessed before the United States Congress to having been given the answers to the questions on the show "Twenty-One".

He resigned his position as assistant professor at Columbia University. The scandal was later made into a film called "Quiz Show" directed by Robert Redford with Ralph Fiennes in the role of van Doren (see page 183).

Giving Birth to Rabbits

Born in Surrey in 1701 Mary Toft became famous in 1726 when, craving fame and fortune, she tricked doctors into believing she had given birth to rabbits!

After being examined by several surgeons Toft kept to her story and was taken to London to be examined and eventually, under intense questioning, confessed that the whole story had been untrue. As a result she was imprisoned for fraud but was released without being prosecuted.

The medical profession was held up to ridicule by the public and several surgeons' careers were ended. Many satirical works were produced about this incident and the Wellcome Library in London holds a William Hogarth print of Mary Toft giving birth to the rabbits.

✓ ***"Search for the truth is the noblest occupation of man; its publication is a duty" - Anne Louise Germaine de Stael***

The Land That Never Was

One of the most audacious frauds in history was carried out by one Sir Gregor Macgregor, (pictured right) a flamboyant war hero who had fought as a mercenary in Simon Bolivar's army for independence in South America.

In and around 1822 he offered acreage in Poyais, a new republic on the Caribbean coast of Central America at bargain prices.

He claimed that he had been created a prince of the Principality of Poyais and described the land as a Garden of Eden with rich soil for growing crops and where cotton already grew wild. Saint Joseph, the capital, was he said an efficient, modern town just waiting for investors and developers.

So it was that in 1822 and 1823 two boatloads of settlers left England for Poyais but it wasn't until the immigrants were dumped on the beach that they saw that what they had bought was just swamp. The bond issues, land sales and made up currency had all been a lie.

✓ ***"The trust of the innocent is the liar's most useful tool" - Stephen King***

Before they were able to escape to nearby Belize more than 180 from the original 250 settlers had died of tropical diseases.

When news got back to England, MacGregor fled to France with his wife and two children where he started the hoax all over again. He eventually returned to Venezuela where he was treated as a returning war hero and lived comfortably until his death in 1845.

The Great Salad Oil Swindle

In 1962 Tino De Angelis, a New York commodities trader, started a huge scam to corner the market on soybean oil. He took out massive loans and began buying oil to store in tanks on a farm in New Jersey.

Unfortunately the tanks were increasingly filled with water with only a small amount of oil on top. Inspectors tested the oil floating on the top and thought everything was fine and loans were acquired from a subsidiary of American Express, thus "guaranteeing" that the oil was really there.

Eventually the inspectors found the water which resulted in a massive crash on the futures market. In November 1963 De Angelis's company filed for bankruptcy and investors discovered that hundreds of millions were unaccounted for. The two companies who handled the deals on the New York Stock Exchange were suspended from trading.

✓ ***"Honesty consists of the unwillingness to lie to others. Maturity, which is equally hard to attain, consists of the unwillingness to lie to oneself" - Sydney J. Harris***

As it happened the whole debacle was overshadowed by the assassination of John F Kennedy on the 22nd November, 1963.

When the final tally was known it was discovered that The Great Salad Oil Swindle has cost 51 banks about $175 million in total and De Angelis was sentenced to seven years in jail.

On his release, De Angelis was soon involved in another scam, this time a Ponzi scheme, (see page 100) involving Midwest cattle which also collapsed.

The Great Salad Oil Swindle was documented in a book by the same name which won a Pulitzer Prize in 1964 (see page 175).

Joseph "Yellow Kid" Weil

Joseph Weil was born Chicago in 1875 and became such a con man that he is said to have conned people out of over eight million dollars.

Dressing in sophisticated gentleman's attire he conned hundreds of people, including horseplayers who fell for the old wiretap schemes for beating the odds.

The name "Yellow Kid" came from the comic "Hogan's Alley and the Yellow Kid". Weil had worked for some time with a con man named Hogan and automatically took on the second name of the comic pair.

✓ ***"Beat me with the truth, don't torture me with lies" - Author unknown***

In a co-written autobiography Weil said "The desire to get something for nothing has been very costly to many people who have dealt with me and with other con men but I have found that this is the way it works." He also added "When people learn that they can't get something for nothing, crime will diminish and we shall live in greater harmony."

Weil died in Chicago in 1976 at the grand old age of 100.

Sir Francis Drake left a fortune!

Oscar Hartzell was an American con man who, in 1919, started contacting people in Iowa with the surname of Drake saying that the estate of Sir Francis Drake had never been paid out and it had been gathering interest for 300 years. He asked them to invest in his campaign to sue the British government.

Thousands of people sponsored him, even people without the surname of Drake and who did not live in Iowa.

Hartzell moved to London around 1924, supposedly for negotiations with the British Government. In the meantime the FBI investigated the case and reported that Drake's wife had inherited his estate in 1597. Hartzell was sent for trial in 1933 and was convicted of fraud in 1934 and sentenced to 10 years in prison where he died in 1943.

✓ ***"Whenever, therefore, people are deceived and form opinions wide of the truth, it is clear that the error has slid into their minds through the medium of certain resemblances to that truth" - Socrates***

PONZI SCHEMES

A Ponzi scheme or scam is named after Charles Ponzi a famous con man of the 20th century who became notorious for promoting such a scheme back in the 1920's. The scheme is in fact pyramid selling whereby an enterprise pays investors high returns from the proceeds of later investors rather than from the profits of the business. This is fine whilst there are new investors joining the scheme but as the pool of new investors dries up so do the returns.

Although made famous by Charles Ponzi, who emigrated from Italy to the United States in 1903, such schemes have in fact been around since the time of Charles Dickens. Dickens famously wrote about such a scheme in his 1857 novel "Little Dorrit" when the Dorrits lose all their wealth by investing in Mr Merdle's bank.

It is estimated that in 2009 more than $16 billion of investors' money was lost in Ponzi schemes. The most famous included Bernard Madoff's (see page 102) and Sir Allen Stanford's (see page 103) which overshadowed many other smaller schemes.

Many people have quoted Social Security payments as a Ponzi scheme – those people who paid in first have received payments from those who paid in later. This has worked so far but as an older, larger, population is supported by a smaller workforce this system will eventually collapse and need a bail-out.

✓ ***"There are two ways to be fooled: One is to believe what isn't so; the other is to refuse to believe what is so" - Soren Kierkegaard***

The Original Ponzi Scheme

An Italian swindler, Charles Ponzi is considered to be one of the greatest swindlers of all times and the term "Ponzi Scheme" is now a well known description for any scheme which pays early investors returns from the investments of later investors, very similar to today's pyramid schemes.

Born in 1882 Charles Ponzi (left) emigrated to America at the age of 21 and came to prominence in the 1920's when he set up The Security Exchange Company promising clients that he could double their investment in three months. With flair and media know-how he played the scheme for all it was worth and became a prominent figure in American criminal history. After being apprehended in Florida, Ponzi fled to Texas where he was eventually sent to jail with debts of $7,000,000.

On his release he was deported back to Italy at the age of 52 and died in the charity ward of a Rio de Janeiro hospital in 1949 at the age of 67.

One of the greatest exponents of the Pontzi scheme would be Bernard Mandoff who, in 2009, was sentenced to 150 years in jail for similar activities (see next page).

✓ ***"He who seeks to deceive will always find someone who will allow himself to be deceived" – Machiavelli***

Sentenced to 150 years

One of the largest frauds of all time was committed by the former American stock broker, investment adviser and non-executive Chairman of the NASDEQ stock market, Bernard Madoff.

Born in 1938, Madoff had for decades run a multi-billion dollar Ponzi scheme, which is similar to pyramid selling, described as a deception that was the longest, widest and deepest Ponzi scheme in history. Delivering such hefty returns the Ponzi scheme eventually attracted HSBC who invested a billion dollars in it.

In 2009 Madoff pleaded guilty to 11 federal crimes and of defrauding investors of $65 billions in the investment scam. With losses in the region of $50 billion Madoff admitted that "it's just one big lie" - a lie which triggered suicides and business closures.

That same year Madoff was sentenced to the maximum sentence of 150 years in a federal prison. His lawyers had originally wanted a sentence of just 7 years because of their client's age.

No-one ever really found out why Madoff, a well respected multi-millionaire and philanthropist, would start such a scheme in the first place, one which destroyed friends and charities.

✓ ***"We are often unprepared for Truth, which is why Truth is revealed to us progressively" - Chip Brogden***

Allen Stanford

A financier and philanthropist, Allen Stanford is at the moment in prison waiting trial for a massive Ponzi scheme and fraud. In 2009 Stanford, the Chairman of the now defunct Stanford Financial Group, was charged with fraud involving $8 billion. The FBI raided three of Stanford's offices and in 2009 the Securities and Exchange Commission amended the charge to a "massive Ponzi scheme." Stanford faces 21 charges at his trial which is due to begin in January, 2012.

Backstreet Boys Creator

In 2006 investigators found that the impresario Lou Pearlman had been operating a long running Ponzi scheme and had defrauded investors out of $300 million. Creator of the American vocal group Backstreet Boys, for over 20 years Pearlman had been asking people to invest in Trans Continental Airlines Travel Services Inc. and Trans Continental Airlines Inc., unfortunately there was a snag - they only existed on paper. Pearlman had produced fraudulent documents purported to have come from various companies such as Lloyd's of London and a fictitious accounting firm.

In 2007 Pearlman was arrested in Indonesia and charged with bank fraud, mail fraud and wire fraud and was jailed for 25 years. At the age of 53 this was, in fact, a life sentence for Pearlman who had swindled American banks and investors to put money into fake companies. Pearlman had defrauded almost 2,000 investors, many of whom were pensioners who lost their life savings.

✓ ***"Speak the truth, but leave immediately afterwards" - Slovenian Proverb***

Ponzi Scheme Gets Petters 50 Years

Businessman, Tom Petters, is more than likely to spend the rest of his life in jail for his $3.65 billion Ponzi scheme which was one of the largest in the history of the United States, second only to Bernard Madoff.

At the age of 52 the 50 year prison sentence he was given, the longest ever given for a financial fraud case in Minnesota history, means he received a virtual life sentence. Petters and his business partners told investors that they needed money to purchase electronics but instead diverted the funds to make payments to other investors – the whole idea behind a Ponzi scheme.

The FBI began their investigation in 2008 after a tip-off from a co-conspirator, who said she had been helping Petters run a multi-million dollar Ponzi scheme for ten years. A year later he was convicted, his lawyer arguing that the sentence should have been only 4-12 years.

$813 million scam

One of the largest and longest running scams was operated by James ("Jim") Paul Lewis, Jr. in the United States. Over almost 20 years Lewis collected around US$311 million from his unregistered Financial Advisory Consultants company in California.

Using the classic "Ponzi scheme" the funds from new investors got redistributed to earlier investors.

✓ ***"When a man who is honestly mistaken hears the truth, he will either quit being mistaken, or cease to be honest" - Unknown***

Whilst there were new investors Lewis was able to cover his tracks but when he failed to find any new investors the whole scam came to light.

In 2003 investors failed to receive a dividend and became suspicious and the FBI started to investigate him. Lewis was duly arrested in 2004 and in 2006 was sentenced to 30 years in prison, the statutory maximum. The judge described the scheme as "a crime against humanity" because so many elderly investors has been left destitute. Although ordered to pay US$156 million in restitution, the court appointed receiver has only recovered US$11 million.

✓ ***"The greatest friend of truth is time, her greatest enemy is prejudice, and her constant companion humility" - Chuck Colson***

DEADLIER THAN THE MALE

Although confidence tricksters are usually called "con men" two women in particular have shown that women can also be a force to be reckoned with:

Cassie L Chadwick
Born Elizabeth Bigley in Canada in 1857 Cassie Chadwick went on to defraud several American banks out of millions of dollars by pretending to be the illegitimate daughter and heiress of Andrew Carnegie, the Scottish-American industrialist. Her life of fraud started at the tender age of 13 when she opened a bank account with a forged letter from an unknown uncle. She was arrested for the first time that same year.

Moving to America she married the first of her three husbands. In 1889 she again resorted to forgery and was sentence to nine and a half years in a prison in Ohio but was paroled after four years and later opened a brothel. There she met and married her third husband Dr Chadwick in 1897 and took the name for which she was to become famous, Cassie Chadwick.

It was then that she began her largest and most successful con game – stating that she was the daughter of Andrew Carnegie. The scam began when she "accidentally" dropped a promissory note for $2 million, apparently signed by Carnegie, in front of a lawyer acquaintance.

✓ ***"It is better to be divided by truth than to be united in error" - Adrian Rodgers***

She claimed that she was Carnegie's illegitimate daughter and that he felt so guilty about his secret that he was showering her with money such as the $7 million in promissory notes already in her possession, plus the $400 million she was to inherit on his death.

As the details leaked out to the financial markets she used her fake background to obtain huge loans totaling between $10-$20 million and her lavish lifestyle earned her the title "The Queen of Ohio." In 1904, however, one of the bankers called in his loan and the whole scam was eventually revealed. The Citizen's Bank of Oberline which had loaned her $800,000 suffered a run and was eventually forced into bankruptcy.

Cassie Chadwick was sent for trial in 1905 and was sentenced to 14 years in prison where her health deteriorated and she suffered a collapse in 1907 which left her blind. She died on her birthday in 1907 whilst still in prison, aged 50.

Murderess and Con Artist

The second woman "More Deadlier Than The Male" was Sante Kimes. Born in 1934 she was an American con artist who was also convicted of committing three murders.

Kimes had spent most of her life operating elaborate con games. She committed insurance fraud by arson and also offered young, homeless illegal immigrants housing and then threatened to expose them. She spent years defending herself against slavery charges but was eventually arrested in 1985 and sentence to 5 years.

✓ ***"There is nothing so powerful as truth, and often nothing so strange" – Daniel Webster***

After her release, Kimes and her son, Kenny, were thought to have brutally killed an Indian banker and dumped his body in the sea when he refused her a loan.

The second murder was that of David Kazdin, a family friend, who threatened to expose her previous misdeeds. He had been shot and left in a dumpster near Los Angeles airport.

Her last victim was her landlady, Irene Silverman, whose identity she would assume and obtain ownership of her $7.7 million Manhattan mansion.

Although Silverman's body was never found both Sante and her son Kenny were convicted of murder in 2000 because of Kimes notebooks detailing the crime together with various notes Silverman had written about her suspicions of the pair. Both are serving life sentences.

An autobiography by Kent Walker, Sante Kimes' older son, was published entitled "Son of a Grifter: The Twisted Tale of Sante and Kenny Kimes, the Most Notorious Con Artists in America". It became a best seller and won the Edgar Allan Poe Award in 2002.

✓ ***"We are apt to shut our eyes against a painful truth. For my part, I am willing to know the whole truth; to know the worst; and to provide for it" - Patrick Henry***

FRAUD AND FORGERY

Fraud

According to the Collins English dictionary, fraud is "the deliberate deception, trickery or cheating intended to gain an advantage." Although fraud involves deception and dishonesty there is, in actual fact, no definition of fraud in English law. The act of fraud can cover a whole range of activities from minor offences, credit card fraud, complicated financial transactions and identity fraud. Also, in law, fraud has to be a particular form of lying. Take for instance the case of a salesman – he can lie about his personal details etc but he must not lie about the product he sells.

The effects of fraud can be devastating to the victim whether it is committed face-to-face, by telephone, in a chain letter or on line.

In October 2010 the National Fraud Authority, which helps fight fraud in the UK, stated that, in the first year of Action Fraud, over £78 million of fraud had been reported to them. The Chief Executive did, however, state that more than £3.5 billion is lost by individuals each year and could be much higher but many victims of fraud never report it.

There are, of course, many slang names for fraud such as scam, con, bamboozle and cheat, and these slang terms hide just as much serious crime as the word fraud itself. Many of the above come into their own with the use of the internet which uses e-mailing to attempt to extort money from internet users.

✓ ***"Rather than love, than money, than fame - give me truth" - Thoreau***

The scammers make the public 'dream' that they will receive a percentage of a big money transaction which never materialises.

Phishing - is one of the largest Internet related scams which tries to obtain passwords and credit card details by sending out e-mails supposedly coming from reputable firms, some even from the King of Nigeria.

419 scams - where individuals are sent notification that they have either won money or will obtain a percentage of a large amount of money belonging to a dead or missing individual sharing the same name. Individuals are tricked in to paying large sums of money to help facilitate the transfer of funds. The term 419 is derived from the number in the Nigerian Penal Code corresponding to this type of fraud.

Forgery

Forgery is an intentional deception which has been made for personal gain such as altering a cheque or a document. A law covering forgery has been enshrined in English law since 1861. It is classified as a crime and a civil law violation and is another form of lying. Forgery has always been big business ranging from a forged Roman imperial decree called The Donation of Constantine (see page 114), William Ireland and his forged Shakespeare papers (see page 73) to the Hitler Diaries published a few years ago (see page 67). As with fraud, forgery has many aspects ranging from counterfeiting to art forgery. They are all crimes in law, and are punished severely, particularly in the case of counterfeiting.

✓ ***"We know the truth, not only by the reason, but also by the heart" - Blaise Pascal***

Usually counterfeiting is used to refer to replicating currency but it can also refer to anything from the production of imitation handbags etc to legal documents.

Although there are many kinds of forgery, The Forgery and Counterfeiting Act 1981 quite obviously links the counterfeiting of notes and coins under the same Act and counterfeiting money is treated as a very serious crime around the world. On the other hand the counterfeiting of goods is viewed much more leniently in many countries, some even thinking of counterfeiters as modern day Robin Hoods.

The one common denominator which connects fraud, forgery and counterfeiting is that they are all based on deception and lies.

✓ ***"Truth always rests with the minority, and the minority is always stronger than the majority, because the minority is generally formed by those who really have an opinion, while the strength of a majority is illusory, formed by the gangs who have no opinion—and who, therefore, in the next instant (when it is evident that the minority is the stronger) assume its opinion ... while Truth again reverts to a new minority" - Soren Kierkegaard***

NOTORIOUS FORGERS

Before the nineteenth century it was almost impossible to detect art forgeries but over the last century, with the discovery of scientific techniques, it has become relatively easy to detect a forgery and, as a consequence, the following are just some of the forgeries which have come to light.

The Greatest of Them All

Born in 1889, Hans van Meegeren was considered to be the greatest art forger of all time. Whilst he did not copy great paintings and try to pass them off as his own, he "created" new works of art - the speciality of Meegeren was Vermeer. In all he created six new Vermeer's and marketed them as new discoveries and in the process he amassed a fortune in today's currency of half a billion dollars.

Van Meegeren developed an aging process for his pictures which was practically impossible to distinguish from the real thing. His most famous forgery was "Emmaus" which was purchased by an art museum in Holland and for years was considered the finest Vermeer ever produced.

Shortly after the conclusion of World War II in 1945 van Meegeren was arrested for having sold a Vermeer to Hermann Goering and, afraid that he might be accused of collaboration, he confessed to forgery. He also admitted the forgery of the famous "Emmaus" and several other fakes by famous painters.

Van Meegeren died in December 1947 just before serving a year's sentence for forgery.

✓ ***"When truth is divided, errors multiply" – Eli Siegel***

Shaun Greenhalgh
Born in 1961, Greenhalgh is the British art forger who from 1989 to 2006 with the help of his brother and parents sold his fake paintings to galleries and museums and made himself a millionaire. Scotland Yard described the family as "possibly the most diverse forgery team in the world".

When Greenhalgh was eventually found out he was sentenced to over four years in prison in 2007.

Unusually, the Victoria and Albert Museum held an exhibition of his forgeries in 2010 and the Metropolitan Police built a replica of his workshop and called him "the most diverse art forger known in history".

Lothar Malskat
A German painter and art restorer, Malskat was commissioned to carry out restoration work in two European cathedrals but found it simpler to whitewash over the original paintings and paint completely new pictures on the walls.

His fraud was only discovered when it was noticed that in his "restored" Medieval works he had included a picture of a modern film actress. Malskat was arrested and charged in 1954 and was sentenced to 18 months in prison. The paintings were later washed off the walls.

Malskat died in Lubeck, Germany, in 1988.

✓ ***"Truth, though it has many disadvantages, is at least changeless. You can always find it where you left it" - Phyllis Bottome***

The Donation of Constantine

This is a forged Roman imperial decree which stated that the emperor Constantine I had transferred all authority over Rome and the western part of the Roman Empire to the Bishop of Rome. (pictured left)

The Donation particularly applies to Pope Sylvester I who had converted Constantine to Christianity and had also cured him of leprosy. As Constantine had fought long and hard to unite the empire it is highly unlikely that he would have given such a large part of it away and even the Roman Catholic Church admits it is a forgery.

It is estimated that the document was created between 750 and 850 but that it was not exposed as a forgery until 1440.

Vrain-Denis Lucas

Trained as a law clerk, the French forger Vrain-Denis Lucas began forging historical documents, especially letters, in and around 1854. Collecting details from the Imperial Library he used writing material and ink from the appropriate period and started producing letters from historical figures.

✓ ***"Once your soul has been enlarged by a truth, it can never return to its original size" - Blaise Pascal***

One of the letters, produced in 1861, purported to come from Blaise Pascal saying that he had discovered the laws of gravity. As this would have meant that a Frenchman had discovered gravity before an Englishman they were readily accepted.

Over a period of 16 years Lucas forged thousands of letters, including ones from Mary Magdalene, Pontius Pilate, and Cleopatra etc. Slowly however the French Academy of Science began to notice discrepancies in historical facts and handwriting samples.

In 1869 Lucas was arrested for forgery and in 1870 he was sentenced to two years imprisonment. Lucas later disappeared from the public eye.

✓ ***"The thought that provokes thought is much more valuable than the thought that is only an echo of an accepted truth" - Thomas W. Hanford***

THE BIBLE

The Bible gives frequent warnings about lies and repeatedly states that they are the work of the devil. Jesus tells his disciples "I am the way, the TRUTH and the life" (St. John, Chapter 14, verse 6), and although not actually using the word "lie" the Bible has the issue well and truly covered with the ninth commandment which states "Though shalt not bear false witness"(Exodus Chapter 20, verse16).

Adam and Eve in the Garden of Eden

The very first lie every told was when Satan tempted Eve in the Garden of Eden. This was why Christ would later refer to Satan as "the father of lies" (St John, Chapter 8, verse 44). The Bible tells the story of how the devil disguised himself as a serpent and tempted Eve to eat from the tree of life. Eve told him that she and Adam could eat from any tree in the garden except that one, telling him what God had said – that if they ate from that tree they would die. Satan knew this but lied and said "You will not die." Eve, believing Satan, ate from the tree and gave some of the fruit to Adam. As a result, God cast them out of the Garden of Eden and denied them access to the tree of life which would have allowed them to live for ever and from that day they began to die.

✓ ***"Truthful lips will be established forever, but a lying tongue is only for a moment" – Proverbs 12, v.19***

One interesting feature of the story is that we always think of the fruit in the Garden of Eden story as being an apple, but there is no mention in the Bible of an apple. It was more probably a fig as Adam and Eve are often depicted wearing fig leaves.

Jacob lies to Isaac in order to receive his blessing

As Isaac, the son of Abraham, was very old he realized he must give his formal blessing to the son he wanted to succeed him. He had twin sons Esau and Jacob – Esau was his favourite son who was good at hunting, physically strong and confident, whereas Jacob was quiet, thoughtful and intelligent.

In Hebrew tribes the blessing was much prized and it meant the handing over of legal power. The person who received the blessing would rule the whole clan. Isaac very much wanted to give the blessing to Esau but his wife had other ideas and favoured Jacob.

Isaac was old, and his eyesight was very poor when he asked Esau to go out into the field for some venison and make him his favourite dish and then he would bless him. Isaac's wife, Rebekah, heard what was happening and told Jacob and between them they plotted to make the dish themselves and pretend it was made by Easu.

✓ ***"Our first decision about Truth is based upon who Jesus is. With that question settled many Christians are content, but Truth is living. Truth will continue to reveal Himself to us and around us for as long as we will allow it" - Chip Brogden***

Jacob had his doubts though, as he said to his mother, "Esau my brother is a hairy man and I am a smooth man. My father will feel my arms and know that I am not Easu." His mother was not to be deterred and made Jacob cover himself with the skins of some goats so that when his father, Isaac, touched him he would be deceived. (right, Isaac blessing Jacob)

When the venison stew was ready, Jacob took the dish to Isaac and lied to him saying "I am Esau your first born; I have done as you asked." Isaac stretched out his hands and felt Jacob skin which was covered in goats' hair and, feeling the roughness believed that Jacob was in fact Esau and gave him his blessing. (Genesis Chapter 17, verses 1-29).

When Esau returned and found out what had happened he begged Isaac to bless him as well but Isaac told him "I can't, your brother has tricked me and he has stolen your blessing." From that day on Esau hated his brother Jacob.

Joseph and the lies of Potiphar's wife

Joseph was Jacob's son and Jacob loved him very much and gave him a wonderful coat of many colours. Unfortunately Joseph's older brothers were so jealous of him that they plotted to kill him.

✓ ***"Lie not one to another" - Colossian Chapter 3, v.9***

At the last moment, however, they decide instead to throw him into a pit and later sold him to some travelling merchants so that they would never have to see him again.

When the caravan of travelling merchants arrived in Egypt they sold Joseph to a man named Potiphar who was the captain of the palace guard in Pharaoh's court. Potiphar was so pleased with the way Joseph worked that he made him his personal servant. Potiphar's wife, however, was so taken with Joseph that she tried to seduce him on numerous occasions but Joseph remained loyal to Potiphar.

One day, in desperation, she grabbed Joseph's coat and, as he ran away, he left his coat in her hands. (left, Joseph and Potiphar's wife)

Potiphar's wife was furious at his rejection and lied to her husband accusing Joseph of molesting her, saying "Look, he ran away so fast he left his coat behind". Her husband had Joseph put in prison (Genesis Chapter 39). It was whilst he was in prison that Joseph interpreted some dreams of Pharaoh about the future when there would be seven years of plenty followed by seven years of famine. As a result Pharaoh put Joseph in charge of food management and he became the second most powerful man in Egypt after Pharaoh.

- ✓ ***"A false witness shall not be unpunished, and he that speaketh lies shall not escape" - Proverbs Chapter 19, verse 5.***

Peter lies three times

One of the most famous lies in the Bible was told three times by Peter. Jesus had gone to the Garden of Gethsemane with his disciples to pray after the last supper. Whilst there he was betrayed by one of his own disciples, Judas Iscariot, who had told the Temple Guards that, for the payment of 30 pieces of silver, he would lead the guards to Jesus.

As a result, Jesus was taken back to Jerusalem and accused of blasphemy by the leaders of the Pharisees and was subsequently condemned to death (below-Jesus is arrested).

Afraid that the same fate may befall them the disciples scattered but Peter was recognized three times and three times he denies knowing Christ. Later Peter recalls the words of Jesus who had said "Before the cock crows you will deny me three times."

Peter had not believed that he would ever deny his Christ and when he realized what he had done, and heard the cock crow; he went out and wept bitterly. (Matthew, Chapter 26, verses71-75)

✓ ***"From the cowardice that shrinks from new truth; from the laziness that is content with half-truths; from the arrogance that thinks it knows all truth – oh God of Truth deliver us" - Unknown***

King Herod lies about wanting to worship Jesus

Herod, king of Judea, heard the rumour that three Magi were asking to see Jesus, who had just been born in Bethlehem, saying "Where is he that is born king of the Jews for we have seen his star in the east and are come to worship him." (Matthew Chapter 2, verse2). Herod listened to the rumours with fury afraid this new "king" was a threat to him so he lied to the Magi saying "Go and search diligently for the young child; and when ye have found him, bring me word again, that I may come and worship him also."

(left - Herod)

After the Magi had found Jesus they were warned in a dream to ignore Herod's request as he wanted to kill the child.

Herod was furious when he realized that the Magi had not returned and sent his soldiers to Bethlehem to kill all the children under than two years of age thinking Jesus would certainly be one of the ones killed. But God had warned Joseph in a dream to get out of harm's way so Joseph took Mary and Jesus to live in Egypt where they would be safe.

Joseph, Mary and Jesus stayed in Egypt until Herod died, and then returned to Nazareth. (St. Mathew, Chapter 2)

✓ ***"Thou shalt not raise a false report: put not thine hand with the wicked to be an unrighteous witness" – Exodus, Chapter 23, verse 1***

Thomas Jefferson on lies and the Bible

One of the most famous people who concluded that the Bible contains lies and intentional untruths was Thomas Jefferson.

Jefferson (pictured right) was the third President of the United States from 1801-1809 and the principal author of the Declaration of Independence.

He edited his own version of the Bible, called "The Life and Morals of Jesus of Nazareth" published in 1895 which is still in print today. In compiling what has now come to be known as "The Jefferson Bible" he omitted all that he thought to be falsehoods.

In describing the Bible, Jefferson wrote "so much untruth, and falsifications".

There is some irony, however, in the fact that the Jefferson Memorial has a carved panel on his marble walls which proclaims Jefferson's boast "I have sworn eternal hostility against every form of tyranny over the mind of men" and yet he was a slave owner.

✓ ***"God offers to every mind its choice between truth and repose. Take which you please; you can never have both" - Ralph Waldo Emerson***

POLITICIANS

When looking at the history of the lie it will come as no great surprise to find that politicians provide a really rich seam! The particular form this rich seam takes is usually the "noble lie" which is an untruth or a myth knowingly told by politicians for the "good of the country".

A lie may be for the purpose of national security or to protect lives in a security operation where hostages are involved, or in a time of war, but more often than not a deliberate lie, told by a politician or public official, can have a more sinister motive. It seems to be an inescapable fact that leaders of nations will lie, even to the extent of taking their country into a war that the public would have refused to sanction. Of course lies can only become famous because of the famous person who utters them.

Leo Strauss, (pictured right), specialized in classical political philosophy and he noted that way back as far as Plato, thinkers had raised the problem of whether good politicians could be completely truthful and still achieve their goals.

✓ ***"People always have been, and they always will be, stupid victims of deceit and self-deception in politics" - Lenin***

Strauss firmly believed that policy advisers had to deceive their own people in order to protect their country.

He had the idea that there was always a hidden meaning and that lies are the norm in political life, in other words – what politicians say is not always what they do!

Almost all politicians are guilty of St. Augustine's lie No. 5 which says "That lie which is told from a desire to please others in smooth discourse." The author, Charles Ford, states that "politicians are mouthpieces for the self-deception of the people. Wittingly or unwittingly, they tell us that which we have asked them to tell us." They will often try to bamboozle the public with statistics as statistics can say almost anything you want them to say.

✓ ***"I am different from Washington; I have a higher, grander standard of principle. Washington could not lie. I can lie, but I won't" - Mark Twain***

AMERICAN PRESIDENTS

As mentioned in the introduction, Bella DePaulo, of the University of Virginia at Charlottesville, USA, has done several studies on lying and says "no one is totally honest all the time." In one of her studies, published in the Journal of Personality and Social Psychology, she revealed that people told at least one lie a day, and that the more socially adept amongst us stretched the truth more often than the less socially adept.

In 1932 Jean Piaget, an eminent Swiss psychologist, wrote "The tendency to tell lies is a natural tendency, spontaneous and universal." In the end, Presidents lie for the same reason everyone else does, it's just that the rest of us don't get found out quite so publicly.

We all know the apocryphal tale told by Mason Locke Weems generally known as Parson Weems, an American book agent and author about the young George Washington (pictured above) who he said could not lie.

✓ ***"I am a firm believer in the people. If given the truth, they can be depended upon to meet any national crisis. The great point is to bring them the real facts." - Abraham Lincoln***

The story goes that George Washington, when questioned by his father, supposedly confessed to cutting down a cherry tree with the famous phrase, "I cannot tell a lie." This very famous tale is included in "The Life of Washington" published in the 1800's which was Weems' most famous work. The nineteenth century best seller set out to show Washington's many virtues and give moral instruction to the young people of a very young nation.

This story just goes to show how much the Americans respected their first President and their belief that this honesty should apply to the Presidency.

Unfortunately, when looking at the history of the lie, their belief was never going to be and American Presidents in particular seem to feature quite a lot in the history of the lie. Their lies started as far back as 1898 with President William McKinley, the 25th President, although it wasn't until the television age that Presidents were held accountable and had to answer to the Supreme Court for any lies they told.

Watergate was, of course the most famous of all Presidential lies. In a national poll held in 1976, 70% of Americans agreed that their leaders had persistently lied to them in one way or another.

This was a far cry from the nation who believed in Parson Weems' tale about the young George Washington, who became their revered first President, being unable to lie. Those were the days when Presidents did not have to face the full force of the media or a grand jury.

- ✓ ***"I don't mind lying, but I hate inaccuracy" - Samuel Butler***

Whilst there have been many Presidents who have had many uncomfortable questions to answer, it wasn't until 1970's that a President would face an official enquiry.

Some of the more questionable cases of statements by American Presidents which were never actually brought before the Supreme Court were as follows:

President William McKinley, 25th President of the United States (1897–1901), told the American people in 1898 that the USS Maine had been sunk in Havana Harbour by a Spanish mine with the loss of some 250 American sailors.

They were so outraged by this apparent unprovoked attack that they supported the Spanish American War.

The Captain of the USS Maine had insisted the ship was sunk by a coal bin explosion and investigations after the war proved that this had, in fact, been the case. There had been no mine.

✓ ***"You can fool some of the people all the time, and all of the people some of the time, but you cannot fool all of the people all the time" - Abraham Lincoln***

President F D Roosevelt, 32nd President of United States (1933–1945), claimed that Pearl Harbour was a surprise attack on the American fleet on 7th December 1941, the attack which resulted in the United States entry into World War II.

Official records of intercepted Japanese transmissions prove that FDR knew of the attack on Pearl Harbour, and internal Navy documents show that Pearl Harbour was the hoped-for result of a programme of harassment designed to provoke Japan into an attack. There are numerous accounts of actions by Roosevelt and his top armed forces advisors, which reveal they were not only aware of an attack by Japan but were planning on it and, in fact, instigated it.

On the 25 November, 1941, ten days before the attack on Pearl Harbour, the Secretary of War, Henry L Stimson, wrote in his diary, after a meeting of the War Cabinet, the famous statement that he had met with President Roosevelt to discuss the evidence of impending hostilities with Japan, and the question was "how we should manoeuvre the Japanese into the position of firing the first shot without allowing too much danger to ourselves."

✓ ***"In warfare, truth is so precious that she should always be attended by a bodyguard of lies" – Winton Churchill***

President Harry S Truman, 33rd President of the United States (1945–1953) famously lied to the American people about his motives for dropping two atomic bombs, one on Hiroshima on 6 August 1945 and the other on Nagasaki three days later.

In a radio speech on 9 August, 1945 he also lied about the nature of the first target when he gave the following assurance:

"The first atomic bomb was dropped on Hiroshima, which is a military base. This is because we wished in this first attack to avoid, in so far as possible, the killing of civilians." (taken from the Public Papers of the Presidents of the United States).

The bombing was in retaliation for the devastation of Pearl Harbour but Pearl Harbour was a military base whilst Hiroshima was a city inhabited by some three hundred thousand people.

Truman also claimed at various times that Hiroshima was an industrial centre but all the major factories in Hiroshima were on the outskirts of the city and they escaped serious damage.

- ✓ ***"It takes two to lie, one to lie and one to listen" - Homer Simpson!***

President John F Kennedy, 35th President of the United States (1961–1963)

President Kennedy always denied that he had Addison's disease, an incurable disorder of the adrenal glands. The disease named after the British doctor Thomas Addison in 1849.

Kennedy was first diagnosed with Addison's in 1947 by a London physician when he was given less than a year to live. He was in fact one of the best-known Addison's sufferers and one of the first to survive major surgery.

A great deal of secrecy surrounded his health during his years as President. During the 1960 Presidential race, the Kennedy campaign always denied the claim that he had Addison's. It was once claimed to be "undoubtedly one of the most cleverly laid smoke screens ever put down around a politician." Although there was a public record of his illness at the time, which would have uncovered the lie, no-one revealed the truth which would almost certainly have prevented Kennedy becoming a candidate, much less the President of the United States.

✓ ***"The truth that makes men free is for the most part the truth which men prefer not to hear" - Herbert Sebastien Agar***

It was, in part, as a result of this secrecy that the 25th amendment to the United States Constitution was first mooted. Although the Constitution had provided for the succession on the death of a President it had not catered for the disability of a President. The Amendment provides the following remedies when a President is disabled: One is that the President, of his own accord, passes Presidential power to the Vice President. The second remedy is that the Vice President, with the consent of a majority of the cabinet, may make himself acting President on a temporary basis.

The 25th Amendment was finally ratified in 1967.

President Lyndon Baines Johnson, 36th President of the United States, (1963–1969).
On 2 August 1964, naval forces of the United States and North Vietnam skirmished in the waters of the Gulf of Tonkin. Just two days later, the USS Maddox reported a further engagement with North Vietnamese torpedo boats.

Upon the news of the second clash, it took a mere three days for Congress to pass the Gulf of Tonkin Resolution, which stated that President Lyndon B. Johnson could give aid to any Asian country whose government was in harms way of a communist invasion.

✓ ***"It is error alone which needs the support of government, truth can stand by itself" - Thomas Jefferson***

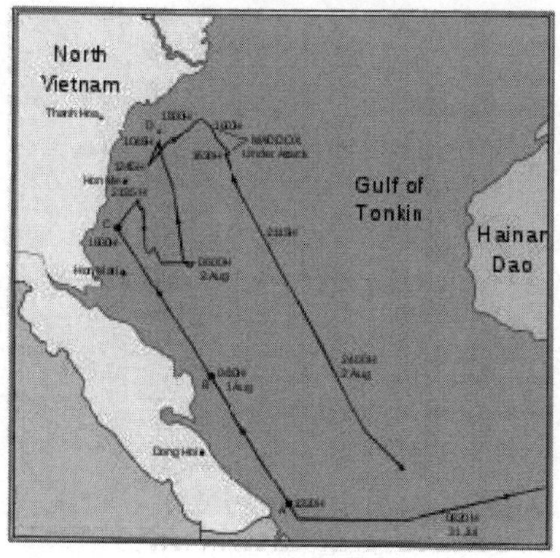

Recently, the National Security Agency, declassified over 140 formerly top secret documents on the August 1964 Gulf of Tonkin incident. Included in these documents were intelligence reports and oral interviews that drove home the point that has long been suspected, but never proven, that there was no second attack on US ships.

President Richard Milhous Nixon, 37th President of the United States (1969–1974) was the only person to be elected twice to both the Presidency and the Vice Presidency. In 1952 in became one of the youngest Vice Presidents in history. Unfortunately he was also the only President to resign.

Nixon was caught in a web of lies in the 1970's, known as the Watergate scandal, which would be forever linked with his name. In the summer before his successful re-election to a second term, five men were caught breaking into the Watergate Hotel because they said they had had information from "a government agency that the Cuban government was supplying funds to the Democratic party".

✓ ***"There can be no public or private virtue unless the foundation of action is the practice of truth" - George Jacob Holyoake***

As details emerged over the next year, it became clear that the Nixon's officials had instigated the break-in. The question was - did Nixon know about the break-in, was he covering it up and had he actually ordered it?

In response to mounting suspicions, Nixon denied all the allegations and told one of the great Presidential lies when he said "I am not a crook." This lie would come back to haunt him. When it was revealed that private White House conversations about the matter were recorded, the investigative committee subpoenaed the tapes. Nixon's refusal on the basis of "executive privilege" brought the matter to the U.S. Supreme Court, which ruled that he had to relinquish the tapes. They revealed that he obviously knew more about the matter than he claimed. Upon the initiation of impeachment proceedings, Nixon resigned from office in 1974.

The scandal left a lasting scar on the American political scene. With the fall of Nixon came the downfall of the following high-ranking officials who would found guilty of perjury:

✓ ***"An honest politician is one who, when he is bought, stays bought" - Lincoln's Secretary of War***

January 1, 1975: John N. Mitchell; former United States Attorney General and director of Nixon's 1966 and 1972 election campaigns. He was found guilty of conspiracy, obstruction of justice, and perjury and was sentenced to between two and eight years in prison.

The sentence was later reduced to one to four years. However Mitchell served only 19 months of his sentence before being released on parole for medical reasons.

January 1, 1975: John Ehrlichman, Nixon's Assistant for Domestic Affairs, was convicted of conspiracy, obstruction of justice, perjury and other charges. He was initially sentenced to between two and eight years in prison. He was released after serving only 18 months.

January 1, 1975: H.R. Haldeman, Nixon's White House Chief of Staff was convicted of conspiracy, obstruction of justice, perjury and other charges. He was initially sentenced to between two and eight years in prison. In 1977, the sentence was commuted to one to four years.

President "Bill" Clinton, **42nd President of the United States** (1993–2001). On 6 May 1994 a young Arkansas state employee named Paula Jones sued President Clinton for sexual harassment stating that he had allegedly propositioned her whilst he had been the then governor of Arkansas. It was whilst the lawyers were trying to find a pattern of such behaviour that his two year affair with another young intern, Monica Lewinsky, came to light.

✓ ***"The simple step of a courageous individual is not to take part in the lie. One word of truth outweighs the world" - Alexander Solzhe***

This affair had lasted 2 years from 1995-1997 whilst Clinton was President of the United States. The lawyers questioned Clinton who, whilst under oath, denied the whole affair. It was later found that Clinton had committed perjury and had obstructed the course of justice which was grounds for impeachment.

There have in fact only been four cases in American history when Congress has seriously discussed the impeachment of a President.

Two such cases were acquitted:

<u>Andrew Johnson</u>, the 17th President (pictured right), in 1868, under the Tenure of Office Act, intended to restrict the power of the President to remover certain office holders without the support of the Senate; and

✓ ***"Get your facts first, then you can distort them as you please" - Mark Twain***

Bill Clinton

In 1999 the impeachment of Bill Clinton by the House of Representatives, which is the political equivalent of a Grand Jury indictment, included a charge that he had committed perjury in testimony about his relationship with White House intern Monica Lewinsky. The Senate found him not guilty of the charge on a 55-45 vote.

One case failed:

John Tyler, the 10th President (pictured right), in 1842, after Tyler vetoed a tariff bill. This was the first impeachment proceedings against a President; and

Richard Nixon, the 37th President who resigned in 1974.

President George W Bush, 43rd President of the United States (2001–2009).

Bush will be forever associated with the war in Iraq. During 2002 and 2003 President George Bush consistently lied about his reasons for wanting to invade Iraq. In various State of the Union Addresses he persistently claimed that Iraq had chemical weapons, a growing fleet of planes and was training al-Qaeda members. It has since been proved that none of this was true.

✓ ***"No man has a good enough memory to make a successful liar" - Abraham Lincoln***

When a President makes a statement on a matter as serious as war it has to be perfectly truthful, he cannot distort facts to gain his own end. President Bush only had to look back at recent history to see what happens to Presidents who lie – President Lyndon Johnson's twisting of the truth about North Vietnam stopped him standing for re-election and President Richard Nixon's false statements about Watergate forced his resignation.

✓ ***"The foulest damage to our political life comes not from the 'secrets' which they hide from us, but from the little bits of half-truth and disinformation which they do tell us" - E.P. Thompson***

ENGLISH POLITICIANS

As with the section on American Presidents there are many questions hanging over various actions of English politicians. Some would argue that politicians should always tell the truth but in 1994 the Conservative MP, William Waldegrave who served in the Cabinet from 1990 – 1997, stated that "In exceptional circumstances it is necessary to say something that is untrue in the House of Commons. The House of Commons understands that and accepts that". This was seized on by the opposition as "sleaze" but it could also be seen as being a rare case of a politician giving an honest answer!

In 1712 the satirist, John Arbuthnot, (pictured left), proposed writing a book entitled "The Art of Political Lying". Although the book was never published Arbuthnot was quoted as saying "the noble and useful art of political lying" and promised to examine whether political lying should be the exclusive right of the government.

The proposed book took the form of a treatise (generally longer and in greater depth than an essay) and proposed a scheme for the Whig party which virtually said that they should speak nothing but the truth for three months, which would give them credit for six months of lying afterwards!

✓ ***"To be persuasive we must be believable; to be believable we must be credible; credible we must be truthful" - Edward R. Murrow***

Funnily enough Arbuthnot's essay was almost a lie in itself as it takes the form of a fake prospectus for a book. (pictured right)

PROPOSALS
For PRINTING
A very Curious Difcourfe, in
Two Volumes in *Quarto*,
Intitled
ΨΕΥΔΟΛΟΓΙ'Α ΠΟΛΙΤΙΚΗ';
OR, A
TREATISE of the Art
OF
Political Lying
WITH
An ABSTRACT of the Firft Volume
of the faid TREATISE.

LONDON

Printed for *John Morphew*, near *Stationers-Hall*. 1712. Price 3d

It has been said that some politicians believe that democratic voters do not always know what is good for them and can only be persuaded by deceit.

In his book "The Rise of Political Lying", Peter Oborne, the Political Editor of "The Spectator" traces the history of political lying back to its origins. It shows how lying, or being "economical with the truth", has become almost acceptable and is part and parcel of modern day politics. From patchy announcements through to blatant falsehoods, Oborne shows how the political lie is always around and has led to such an enormous distrust of our politicians

John Profumo

Although John Profumo was a Brigadier, a Baron, the Secretary of Sate for War and held the OBE he will be forever associated with a 1963 sex scandal, now known as the Profumo Affair, which contributed to the downfall of the Conservative government under the leadership of Harold Macmillan.

✓ ***"The highest truth cannot be put into words" - Lao tzu.***

Profumo had denied allegations by fellow MP's that he was involved with Christine Keeler, who was also involved with an attaché from the Russian Embassy. In a letter to Harold Macmillan, Profumo had stated that there had been no impropriety in the association. He later had to admit the affair to the House of Commons on the 22 March 1963, stating "To my very deep regret I have to admit that this was not true, and that I misled you and my colleagues and the House." After his resignation, Profumo devoted the rest of his life to volunteer work and was eventually made a fundraiser. He was awarded a CBE in 1975 and died 9 March, 2006 at the age of 91.

Jonathan Aitken

Jonathan Aitken, born in 1942, was a former Conservative Member of Parliament who in 1999 was accused of an arms deal scam with the Saudis. He vehemently denied this claim and, in denouncing the allegations of "The Guardian" newspaper, came out with his famous remark "It falls to me to start a fight to cut out the cancer of bent and twisted journalism in our country with the simple sword of truth and the trusty shield of British fair play…."

In the court case which followed it was discovered that Aitken had lied to the High Court, to the Prime Minister and also the Cabinet Secretary and had got his wife to lie and give him an alibi.

Aitken was charged with perjury and perverting the course of justice and was jailed for 18 months but was released after just seven months.

✓ ***"In a time of universal deceit, telling the truth is a revolutionary act" - George Orwell***

As the author of a book on Richard Nixon he was later to say about his own case "The actual offence was small. It was a cover up. I should have learned from Nixon's mistake."

Jeffrey Archer

Jeffrey Archer was made a life peer in 1992. He had been an MP and deputy chairman of the Conservative Party, plus an author, actor, and playwright. He has had several brushes with the law.

In 1987 Archer was accused of having sex with a prostitute, Monica Coghlan, and won a libel case against the "Daily Star" to the sum of £500,000 and the editor of the paper was subsequently sacked. However, in the light of further evidence, it was later established, in 2001, that Archer had actually perjured himself at the trial and he was subsequently jailed for four years in 2001. The trial began on 30 May 2001, a month after Monica Coghlan's death in a car crash. When sentencing him, the judge, Mr Justice Potts said "These charges represent as serious an offence of perjury as I have had experience of and have been able to find in the books."

Whilst in prison, Archer wrote a three volume memoir called "A Prison Diary". In 2002 Archer repaid the Daily Star the £500,000 as well as legal costs and interest of £1.3 million.

✓ ***"The truth is the only thing worth having, and, in a civilized life, like ours, where so many risks are removed; facing it is almost the only courageous thing left to do" - E.V. Lucas***

Tony Blair, Prime Minister of the United Kingdom (1997-2007)

Tony Blair strongly supported the United States by joining with them in the invasion of Afghanistan and later Iraq. He justified his actions by stating before Parliament that Iraq was developing WMD's (weapons of mass destruction) and the fact they Saddam Hussein could launch such weapons within 45 minutes. Such weapons have never been discovered.

In 2003 Dr. David Kelly, an employee of the Ministry of Defense and an expert on biological warfare, was found dead, supposedly having committed suicide, after it was revealed that he was the source of quotes used by the BBC which said that Tony Blair and his government had knowingly "sexed up" a report into Iraq's reported WMD's. An inquiry was immediately launched, called the Hutton Inquiry, into the circumstances surrounding the death of Dr. Kelly who had expressed doubts about the legality of the government's invasion of Iraq. The report cleared the government of any wrongdoing.

In 2009 six doctors began a legal action demanding an inquest into Dr. Kelly's death stating "there is insufficient evidence to prove beyond reasonable doubt that he killed himself". For some unexplained reason, Lord Hutton however ordered that all the files should remain secret for 70 years.

In 2010 an enquiry began to investigate the reasons for the war on Iraq. Called the Chilcot Inquiry it is still going on.

✓ ***"The true hypocrite is the one who ceases to perceive his deception, the one who lies with sincerity" - Andre Gide***

In October that same year details of the pathologist's report into Dr Kelly's death were released which stated that his wounds were "self-inflicted".

In 2011 the police admitted that a helicopter had landed at the scene of Dr Kelly's death a few minutes after his body had been found and then left within a few moments later. This was never disclosed to the Hutton Enquiry so it is not known if the helicopter collected or delivered anything. Details from the flight log, released under the Freedom of Information Act, had also been heavily redacted.

Unfortunately Dr Kelly's mobile 'phone records were never checked which may have thrown some light onto the truth of the whole episode.

✓ ***"The statesmen will invent cheap lies, putting the blame upon the nation that is attacked, and every man will be glad of those conscience-soothing falsities, and will diligently study them, and refuse to examine any refutations of them; and thus he will by and by convince himself that the war is just, and will thank God for the better sleep he enjoys after this process of grotesque self-deception" - Mark Twain***

MPs Expenses Scandal

It was during Tony Blair's administration that the expenses scandal hit the headlines. In 2009 "The Daily Telegraph" began a series of disclosures which showed that dozens of MP's had been lying about their expenses over a period of years. As a result four former MPs and two Lords – Elliot Morley, David Chaytor, Jim Devine and Eric Illsley - and Lords Hanningfield and Taylor - faced criminal charges.

The MPs had argued that the allegations should be a matter for Parliament and not the courts as they were protected by parliamentary privilege enshrined in the Bill of Rights of 1688. This argument was rejected by Mr. Justice Saunders, a High Court judge, and also by the Court of Appeal who said "In our judgment no question of privilege arises, and the ordinary process of the criminal justice system should take its normal course, unaffected by any groundless anxiety that they might constitute an infringement of the principles of parliamentary privilege."

On 3 December, 2010 the former Labour MP David Chaytor pleaded guilty to three charges relating to his expenses just three days before he was due to stand trial. The 61 year old MP for Bury North was charged with false accounting under the Theft Act. He was the first Parliamentarian due to face trail over his expenses. On 7 January 2011 he was jailed for 18 months for fraudulently claiming more than £20,000 in expenses. His lawyer, James Sturman QC was quoted as saying that Chaytor was "a broken man who had paid a devastating price for his stupidity".

✓ ***"Honesty is the first chapter of the book of wisdom" - Thomas Jefferson***

Chaytor was released from jail after serving just one third of his 18 month sentence.

In February 2011, ex-Labour MP Jim Devine was found guilty on two counts of claiming over £8,000 in expenses by using false invoices. When prosecuting, Mr Peter Wright QC said MPs should be guided by the principles of "selflessness, integrity, objectivity, accountability, openness, honesty and leadership". Devine was sentenced to 12 months imprisonment.

In May 2011 the ex-Labour Environment Minister, Elliot Morley, became the first former Minister to be jailed for cheating on his expenses when he was sentenced to 16 months imprisonment for claiming more than £30,000 in bogus mortgage payments. He entered two guilty pleas for false accounting and was sentenced at London's Southward Crown Court.

The Tory peer, and former frontbencher, Lord Hanningfield was found guilty at Chelmsford Crown Court on six counts of expenses fraud amounting to £14,000. The expenses were for overnight accommodation when most nights he had in fact returned to his home less than 50 miles away by using his chauffeur driven car, provided by Essex County Council.

In January 2011 Lord Taylor of Warwick, the first Conservative black peer, was found guilty at Southward Crown Court of making false expenses claims to the value of more than £11,000 for travel and overnight expenses.

✓ ***"Ambition drove many men to become false; to have one thought locked in the breast, another ready on the tongue" - Sallust***

He was sentenced to 12 months imprisonment at the end of May that same year so becoming the first member of the House of Lords to be jailed over the expenses scandal. When sentencing Mr Justice Saunders said that Lord Taylor was guilty of "a protracted course of dishonesty." He also condemned the lies Lord Taylor has told to cover up his dishonesty.

In May 2011, former Barnsley Central MP Eric Illsley was released from prison after serving three months of a 12 month sentence for expenses fraud amounting to £14,000 relating to a second home. He was sentenced at Southwark Crown Court in February after pleading guilty of three charges..

In July 2011, former Conservative peer, Lord Hanningfield, was jailed for 9 months for falsely claiming nearly £14,000. Passing sentence, Mr Justice Saunders said "Great trust was placed in peers to be honest in their claims. Lord Hanningfield and others have broken that trust".

✓ ***"We cannot afford to differ on the question of honesty if we expect our republic permanently to endure. Honesty is not so much a credit as an absolute prerequisite to efficient service to the public. Unless a man is honest, we have no right to keep him in public life; it matters not how brilliant his capacity" - Theodore Roosevelt***

LYING AND WAR

It has been proved many times that deception in war can be even more deadly than gunfire. The lies deliberately planted to mislead the enemy - as in the case of "The Man Who Never Was" – together with the construction of fake military installations, airfields and the like can be extremely effective. Unfortunately it is a fact of life that many accounts of war are not true. One of the main reasons of course is that history, in the words of Winston Churchill, is written by the victor who seeks to justify a war and therefore the truth is sometimes distorted. War also involves a battle with propaganda and, as a result, it is the propaganda which outweighs honesty.

George Santayana, the Spanish philosopher, once wrote "History is a pack of lies about events that never happened told by people who weren't there." Napoleon Bonaparte put it another way when he said "What is history but a fable agreed upon?"

There are wars which are waged in defence of a human cause which can be justified but there are also, alas, many wars which are imposed on citizens based on lies because of ego and arrogance.

It would be almost impossible to list all the wars throughout the world which have been fought because of lies on one side or the other but a few are mentioned in the section on American Presidents.

✓ ***"Truth: the most deadly weapon ever discovered by humanity. Capable of destroying entire perceptual sets, cultures, and realities. Outlawed by all governments everywhere. Possession is normally punishable by death" - John Gilmore***

Machiavelli, (pictured right) the Italian philosopher, who was born in Florence in 1469, once wrote "never try and win by force that which can be won by deception!"

The word Machiavellian, describing someone who is cunning, devious, unethical, deceiving and dishonest, has even been quoted to describe the decision by George Bush and Tony Blair to invade Iraq.

Adolf Hitler once said "Make the lie big, make it simple, keep saying it, and eventually they will believe it." To prove his point he used this principle of lying to his own people. He told the German people in the 1930's that Poland had attacked first and he staged fake attacks against German targets. The Germans, convinced they were being threatened, followed Hitler into Poland and into World War II.

Likewise the military strategist, Sun Tzu, who lived about 2½ thousand years ago, wrote in "The Art of War" - "All warfare is based on deception." (above - Statue of Sun Tzu).

✓ ***"Peace if possible, truth at all costs" -Martin Luther***

And, as if to prove a point, the motto of Mossad, Israel's intelligence agency which is responsible for intelligence collection, is "By way of deception, thou shalt do war."

The Trojan Horse

As if to illustrate the phrase "never try and win by force that which can be won by deception" the Greeks famously deceived the Trojans when they left them their gift with the words "Citizens of Troy, we present you with this huge wooden horse, as a token of peace between our two countries." In actual fact the war had been raging for 10 years when the Trojans eventually began to think that they had finally overcome the Greeks. They were soon to find out that the Greeks had a very fatal trick to play on them.

The Greeks built the now famous hollow wooden horse in which they could hide their men. They convinced the Trojans that this was a peace offering and it was duly brought into the fortified city.

That night, as the Trojans slept, the Greeks who were hidden inside let themselves out the trap door and proceeded to slaughter the Trojans in their beds. This was unquestionably one of the biggest and most successful lies known in history and the story has won a permanent place in every schoolboy's heart.

✓ ***"If a thousand old beliefs were ruined in our march to truth we must still march on" - Stopford Brooke***

Operation Fortitude

This was the codename for the deception used by the Allied forces in World War II. It was a plan which convinced the Germans that the main invasion of France would be via the Pas de Calais rather than Normandy. Carried out mostly by false wireless transmissions and through Germany double agents it turned out to be one of the most successful, and possibly the most important, deceptions of the war.

Operation Mincemeat

One of the most successful lies of World War II was the wartime plot code named "Operation Mincemeat" better known as "The Man Who Never Was."

In April 1943 the body of a Royal Marines officer was found drifting in the sea off the coast of Spain.

Attached to his wrist was a briefcase containing classified documents wrongly stating that the Allies were planning an invasion of Greece and Sardinia. These documents, as intended, quickly found their way into the hands of the Germans and by May 1943 their troops had been diverted to prevent such an attack.

Two months later the Allies invaded Sicily with very little resistance from the Germans. As a result of the deliberate deception the invasion turned out to be a complete success and made the plan one of the greatest lies of modern times.

✓ ***"Here the ways of men part: if you wish to strive for peace of soul and pleasure, then believe; if you wish to be a devotee of truth, then inquire" - Friedrich Wilhelm Nietzsche***

After the end of the war Operation Mincemeat was found to be one of the most successful military deceptions since the Trojan Horse. It was a member of the general public trawling through the archives who discovered that the body used in the operation was that of a Welsh tramp by the name of Glyndwr Michael, who had committed suicide in London by taking rat poison. In the subterfuge he was to become Captain William "Bill" Martin of the Royal Marines.

In 1953 "The Man Who Never Was" became a book, written by Ewen Montague, which told the whole story of the deliberate deception and later, in 1956, the story was turned into a very successful film staring Clifton Webb.

✓ ***"The victor will never be asked if he told the truth" - Adolf Hitler***

DOUBLE AGENTS IN WORLD WAR II

The life of a double agent is based almost entirely on the ability to lie and such agents have been proved to be the world's best at it. It is their greatest asset but also their worst liability. The countries and organizations the agents work for can never be quite certain if they can trust the agents and, as a result, will often keep them under surveillance. They in turn use double agents to transmit disinformation, in other words "lies". There are of course also triple agents who work for three intelligence services. This is extremely dangerous and is very often life threatening. The background of a triple agent has to be very closely investigated and a network of handlers established. If there is any common denominator in making a good double or triple agent it must be a good sense of self-preservation, the ability to cope with isolation and to live the lie.

In his book "The Dirty War", Martin Dillon covered the whole subject of double and triple agents together with the conspiracies and disinformation between MI5 and MI6 agents.

The First Double Agency of WWII

It was a Welshman, Arthur Owens, who became the very first double agent to be recruited in World War II. He was arrested on the outbreak of war as he was known to have contacts with the German intelligence service.

✓ ***"Be true to yourself and you cannot be a traitor to any good cause on Earth" - Eugene V. Debs***

He was given the codename "Snow", an anagram of his surname. Owens admitted to another double-agent that he was double-crossing MI5; his first interest seemed to be to make money from both sides.

In the end MI5 used Owens' own radio to inform the Germans that he was seriously ill whilst holding Owens in Dartmoor Prison until the end of the war.

At the end of the war Owens emigrated to Canada and threatened to publish his story, demanding compensation for what he called his wrongful arrest in 1941. He was eventually bought off and later moved to Ireland where he died in 1976.

The Double Cross System

This was a World War II deception system, also known as the XX (double cross) System, operated by the British. German agents in Britain were either captured or turned themselves in and were then used by the British to spread disinformation to their German controllers. The operations were overseen by the Twenty Committee, the name being derived from the number 20 in Roman numerals "XX". The success of the Double Cross System meant that it was ideal for strategic deception, culminating in the D-Day deception known as "Fortitude". This plan deceived the Germans into thinking that the Allies would land at Pas de Calais rather than Normandy. Some of the most important double agents during this operation were:

✓ ***"There is no well-defined boundary between honesty and dishonesty. The frontiers of one blend with the outside limits of the other" - O. Henry***

Juan Pujol (codename Garbo), a Spaniard who managed to work for the Germans and the British and was awarded the Iron Cross by the Germans and the MBE by the British;

Dusko Popov, a Yugoslav. Holding anti-Nazi views Popov was working for both MI5 and MI6. In 1941 he obtained information that the Japanese planned to attack Pearl Harbour but nothing was done with it. Popov died in 1981;

Mathilde Carre, a French Resistance agent during World War II, Carre also turned double agent and revealed all the members of the network known to her. Working for the Germans she was sent to London to infiltrate the Special Operations Executive. She was arrested in England and taken to Holloway and then on to Aylesbury prison, becoming an informer against the other prisoners.

After the war Carre was sent back to France and stood trial for treason. She was sentenced to death in 1949 but this was commuted to 20 years imprisonment. Released in 1954 nothing much was heard of her until her death in 1970;

Roman Czerniawski, (codename Brutus) was a Polish Air Force Captain and a double agent of the Allies during World War. Captured by the Germans he was sent over to Britain as a spy and immediately turned himself over to British intelligence;

As a result of the revelations by Mathilde Carre (see above) Czerniawski was arrested and imprisoned.

✓ ***"Friends, if we be honest with ourselves, we shall be honest with each other" - George MacDonald***

Although he was offered safety by the Germans, when he was sent to England he turned into a double agent. He was later instrumental in the Allied deception prior to the D-Day landings in Normandy in 1944 and was one of the primary agents in the execution of Operation Fortitude (see page 150). He died in 1985 at the age of 75.

Eddie Chapman (pictured below) was a wartime double agent and the only Englishman to have been awarded the Iron Cross. His life before the war however was completely at odds with this image.

He was a safe breaker and a crook and whilst awaiting trial in Glasgow he escaped to Jersey where he was again imprisoned when the Germans invaded the Channel Islands. He offered to carry out sabotage for the Germans on the UK mainland and was given the task of blowing up the de Havilland aircraft factory where the new Mosquito fighter bomber was being made. On landing in England he reported to the local police station and said he wanted to pass on information to MI5. Eventually they agreed and he was given the codename "Zig-Zag".

He carried out a mock explosion at the factory, was ordered back to Germany and was awarded the Iron Cross shortly after D-Day.

✓ ***"You never find yourself until you face the truth" - Pearl Bailey***

He was again dropped back into England to report on the damage caused by the V1 and V2 rockets. Where possible he directed them to sparsely populated areas.

The information he sent back to Germany saved the lives of a great number of Londoners.

After the war Chapman got involved in his old ways and wrote a book about his exploits in "The Eddie Chapman Story" published in 1953.

The German Intelligence Chief, Baron Stefan von Grunen, whom Chapman had reported to whilst an agent, attended, the wedding of Eddie's daughter at the end of the war.

Chapman eventually died in St. Albans in 1997.

✓ ***"The modern susceptibility to conformity and obedience to authority indicates that the truth endorsed by authority is likely to be accepted as such by a majority of the people" - David Edwards***

THE CAMERA CANNOT LIE

Unfortunately, with our modern technology and digitally enhanced photographs, the above phrase is no longer true and although generally not considered to be as serious as a lie, the underlying intention of an enhanced photograph is the exactly same. Back in the 19th century however when photographs first became available to the general public it was obvious that whatever picture the camera took was exactly what the camera had seen. The earliest record of the phrase "the camera cannot lie" was in 1895 when it appeared in the "Evening News", Lincoln, Nebraska. Even then there seems to have been doubts about the actual truth of the phrase as the paper actually said "Photographers, especially amateur photographers, will tell you that the camera cannot lie. This only proves that photographers, especially amateur photographers, can, for the dry plate, fib as badly as the canvas on occasion."

Even the phrase "photographic memory" emphasised the exact reproduction of an image but soon photographers began to realise that they could manipulate images to their advantage.

In 1921 a book was published called "The Cruise of the Kawa" relating the travels of Walter E Traprock around the South Pacific. Amongst his many discoveries was a bird which laid square eggs. A picture of the eggs was published in the book with the caption "The camera never lies." The book was an enormous success and Traprock was invited to give lectures about his travels.

✓ ***"All that deceives may be said to enchant" - Plato***

Unfortunately, the book had in actual fact been written by a reporter from "Vanity Fair" who had been commissioned to find out how outrageous a story had to be before its readers stopped believing it.

He was later to comment "Far and wide 'Cruise of the Kawa' was accepted as genuine, frequently even after it had been read".

Cottingley Fairies

This is one of five photographs taken in 1917 in Bradford by two young cousins, Elsie Wright and Frances Griffiths. This one, showing Frances surrounded by the alleged fairies, was one of the photographs used by Arthur Conan Doyle to illustrate an article he had written on fairies and who wanted "to jolt the material 20th century mind out of its heavy ruts in the mud." Although causing some initial interest at the time nothing much more was heard about the photographs after 1921.

Both girls grew up and in 1966 a "Daily Express" reporter traced Elsie who seemed to suggest that she had photographed her thoughts. It was not until 1980 that both of them admitted the photographs were fakes and that they had used cardboard cutouts of fairies.

✓ ***"The man who fears no truth has nothing to fear from lies" - Thomas Jefferson***

The photographs and cameras used are now in the National Media Museum in Bradford.

Loch Ness Monster

The earliest legend about the Loch Ness monster goes back to the time when the Irish monk St. Columba (521-597 AD) is said to have come across the beast when one of his servants was attacked whilst swimming in the lake. In the name of God he commanded the beast to return to the lake and it vanished beneath the water and left the swimmer unharmed.

Although St Columbia (pictured left) had encountered the sea monster some 1400 years before it wasn't until a road was built on the north shore of Lochness around 1933 that Nessie sightings began. The "Daily Mail" decided to hire Marmaduke Wetherell, a famous big game hunter, to investigate and, although he didn't see the monster, he did find some enormous footprints leading into the water.

Unfortunately, when the Natural History Museum examined the tracks they reported that they had been made by a dried hippo's foot, the sort used as umbrella stands! The following year, however, a British surgeon, Colonel Robert Wilson, took a photograph of what appeared to be a serpent in the Loch.

✓ ***"Truth is like the sun. You can shut it out for a time, but it ain't goin' away" - Elvis Presley***

For years the photograph was said to be evidence of the Loch Ness Monster but Wilson refused to have his name used and the photograph became known as "The Surgeon's Photo."

It wasn't until 1994 when a Christian Spurling, at the age of 90, confessed that he, Wetherell and Wilson had "created" the famous photograph. According to Spurling, he and his step-father, Wetherell, had made a model of a serpent, taken it to the Loch and photographed it. The picture had been given to Wilson by Wetherell. Apparently Wetherell had never forgotten his humiliation over the hippo tracks and his son later remembered him saying "We'll give them their monster!"

The Tourist Guy

This was a photograph which went round the world on the internet shortly after 9/11 supposedly from a camera found in the debris of the World Trade Centre.

It shows a man standing on the observation deck of the World Trade Centre minutes before the attack with a jet plane flying just below him and so close to the tower that a collision was inevitable.

✓ ***"The one who buries the Truth in the ground for safekeeping will lose it, while the one who does something with the Truth will receive more Truth. This is why some grow spiritually and some do not" - Chip Brogden***

Eventually a 25 year old Hungarian called Peter Guzli admitted that he was the real tourist and had taken a photograph in 1997. He had then made up the image to show to a few friends who had put it on the internet where it sped around the world. To prove the point he provided the original undoctored photograph together with several others taken at the same time.

✓ ***"The truth that makes us free is always ticking away like a time-bomb in the basement of everybody's church" - Robert Farrar Capon***

LIES IN ADVERTISING

In the 1920's and 30's it was sometimes very difficult to tell the difference been advertising and hoaxes. These days the advertising industry has to adhere to several pieces of legislation such as the Sale of Goods Act 1979, the Supply of Goods and Services Act 1982, the Consumer Protection Act 1987 and the Unfair Terms in Consumer Contracts Regulations 1999. However, some advertisers will use a selection of the following ploys in order to get us to buy their products:

Contextual lies
A contextual lie gives someone a false impression for, although the truth has been told, it has been deliberately taken out of context or exaggerated to such an extent that it gives a false impression;

Economical with the truth
This is a phrase commonly used as a euphemism for deceit and lying, by leaving out important facts and deliberately holding back relevant information. It usually describes using facts but not revealing too much information. It could convey an untrue version of events.

The phrase "economical with the truth" was first known to have been used in the 18th century by the politician Edmund Burke. These days however it is mostly associated with Sir Robert Armstrong, the UK Cabinet Secretary, who used the phrase during the 1986 Australian "Spycatcher" trial which saw the government of the day trying to ban the publication of a book written by a former MI5 employee;

✓ ***"Honesty pays, but it don't seem to pay enough to suit some people" - Frank McKinney Hubbard***

Fabrication
Fabrication is an outright statement, told as a truth, and, although it may be possible or plausible, it is in fact an assumption for which there is no valid proof;

Hyperbole
Hyperbole is really a case of stretching the truth. It means that there is a basis of truth in the statement but the truth has been stretched to make it appear more important than it really is;

Lying by omission
By omitting to tell someone an important piece of information, and deliberately giving a misconception, is lying by omission. It also includes the failure to correct any pre-existing misconceptions.

An example of this is when the seller of a car declares that the car has been serviced regularly but does not mention that a fault was reported at the last service. A prime example of lying by omission is propaganda which is aimed at influencing people by not telling them the full facts;

Misleading or Concealing
Although a misleading statement does not tell an outright lie there is, nonetheless, the intention of getting someone to believe in an untruth. Concealing also has the intention of misleading;

✓ ***"Advertisements contain the only truths to be relied upon in a newspaper" – Thomas Jefferson***

Out of date signage

This category of lie includes any sort of advertisement which still remains after the business concerned has ceased to trade or the use of old stationery which shows out of date information;

Puffery

Puffery is a really exaggerated claim the sort of thing to be found in publicity announcements. Although advertising statements are unlikely to be strictly true in many instances they cannot be proved false and, as a result, do not violate trade laws. Consumers are expected to know that it is not the absolute truth.

✓ ***"The process [of mass-media deception] has to be conscious, or it would not be carried out with sufficient precision, but it also has to be unconscious, or it would bring with it a feeling of falsity and hence of guilt.... To tell deliberate lies while genuinely believing in them, to forget any fact that has become inconvenient, and then, when it becomes necessary again, to draw it back from oblivion for just so long as it is needed, to deny the existence of objective reality and all the while to take account of the reality which one denies all this is indispensably necessary" - George Orwell in the book 1984***

FAKE HALLMARKING

There has been legislation in place governing hallmarking in Britain since 1300 but the modern law is largely comprised in the Hallmarking Act of 1973.

Under the 1973 Act it is an offence to alter a hallmark without the written consent of the Assay Office. If such written consent is given by the Assay Office then the article must have an additional mark showing the year of the alteration. As a result counterfeiters have often tried to alter this mark to make the article look older and, therefore, more valuable than it really is.

Since its formation in 1327 the Worshipful Company of Goldsmiths has played an important part in the regulation of precious metals. It administers the Antique Plate Committee, established in 1939, which looks after the largest known collection of fake and forged antique silver. Articles submitted undergo a series of scientific tests, including silver dating, which is unique to the Assay Office in London.

Peter Ashley-Russell

The biggest silver forger in decades, Peter Ashley-Russell, a serial forger, was sentenced at Snaresbrook Crown Court to 3 years imprisonment in September 2008 for offences under the Forgery Act 2006.

✓ ***"If you want to ruin the truth, stretch it" - Unknown***

He had been behind the faking of hallmarks using imitation punches which he had also forged. These imitation punches would have made tens of thousands of pounds had they not been seized and made the case one of the biggest hallmarking deceptions of the century.

Dr. Robert Organ, Deputy Warden of the Assay Office, London said "This case demonstrates the importance of hallmarking to protect both the consumer and the trade."

Ashley-Russell had a previous conviction for a similar crime when he was sentenced at Blackfriars Crown Court on 16th May 1986.

✓ ***"To seek truth and to utter what one believes to be true can never be a crime. No one must be forced to accept a conviction. Conviction is free" - Michael Servetus***

FAKE POSTAGE STAMPS

1840 saw the first postage stamp issued in Great Britain and by about 1860 the first forgery was on the market. Soon fake stamps were so prolific that a book entitled "Forged Stamps: How to Detect Them" was published.

During World War I forging stamps of Germany, Bavaria and Austro-Hungary was authorised by the UK Government in order to cause economic damage. One of the British Propaganda stamps depicting Himmler is pictured below left.

For their part the Germans also forged a 1935 Silver Jubilee stamp during the war by the order of Himmler, below right.

Jean de Sperati

Sperati was born in Pisa, Italy in 1884 and as a printer and engraver by profession became one of the master forgers of postage stamps in the world, earning him the title "the Rubens of Philately."

✓ ***"One truth out of context can prove very dangerous" - Gregory Phillips***

At his trial in 1948 the French judiciary sentenced him to a year in prison, 10,000 francs fine and 300,000 francs for criminal intentions. Because he was 64 at the time of his trail he did not serve his sentence and in 1954 he sold what remained of his forgeries to the British Philatelic Association for a large sum of money saying that he wanted to stop them falling into the hands of an imitator.

Three years later Sperati died at the age of 73 and now some of his forged stamps are worth more than the originals.

✓ ***"In order that all men might be taught to speak truth, it is necessary that all likewise should learn to hear it." - Dr. Samuel Johnson***

COUNTERFEIT COINS

By the late 1600's English currency was in disarray. Silver coins, which had been made before 1662, had been clipped. This was a process by which the edges of the coins were cut off and the clippings made into new coins. In some cases as much as 9% had been removed from a coin.

After 1662 the Royal Mint protected their coins by engraving, decorating and milling the edges. This didn't, however, stop counterfeiting and by 1696 as much as 10% of the nation's currency was forged.

Although counterfeit coins are covered by the Counterfeiting Act of 1981, in the year 2009/2010 more than 2 million counterfeit coins were returned to the Royal Mint which prompted them to mount a campaign telling people how to spot a fake. Fake coins usually have a poor ribbed edge or a poor design of the Queen.

William Chaloner
A counterfeiter and confidence trickster, Chaloner's career in counterfeiting took him from a poor boy in Warwickshire to a large house in Knightsbridge, London. He was involved in everything from forging "Birmingham Groats", guineas, French pistoles, crowns, bank notes and lottery tickers and in the late 1690's was imprisoned several times.

✓ ***"It is better to ultimately succeed with the truth than to temporarily succeed with a lie" - Adrian Rodgers***

He was renowned for the quality of his work and his successes. In 1725 the Bank of England started producing their £100 bank notes which, to prevent forgery, were printed on official marbled paper.

This did not stop Chaloner who had large stocks of forged blank paper deliver to his Knightsbridge home and began producing his own £100 bank notes.

By January 1699 a complete investigation was in full swing and Chaloner faced two charges of treason – coining French pistoles in 1692 and coining crowns and half-crowns in 1698.

He was found guilty of High Treason and hanged on the gallows at Tyburn in March 1699.

✓ ***"There are three kinds of lies: lies, damned lies, and statistics" – Mark Twain***

IDENTITY THEFT

This is a fraud which is literally a living lie – stealing personal information such as social security numbers, bank details, birth dates etc in order to obtain credit etc and provide a false identity to cover criminal activities.

In the United Kingdom protection of all personal data held by organizations is covered by the Data Protection Act 1998. The Government, together with a variety of organizations which hold such personal data, will increasingly have to better protect the information in their possession.

Although the internet has made identity theft more widespread it has in fact been around for years and the term identity theft was first coined in 1964. Thieves have obtained information from telephone directories and going through peoples' dustbins looking for details from utility bills etc.

With the growth of the internet it is now considered to be the fastest growing crime in the world and, due to the multiple ways that our personal information is stored, is relatively easy for criminals to access. The collection of passwords and personal data is collected by means of spyware, such as a "Trojan horse" which allows criminals to access our computers and hard drives.

✓ ***"Truth and unconditional love will have the final word in reality. This is why right, temporarily defeated, is stronger than evil triumphant" - Martin Luther King***

Marketing agencies make it their business to collect information on our spending habits etc and store this on databases which are constantly being hacked into by unscrupulous characters. Here are some of the statistics:

a) identity fraud is costing the British economy more than £1.7 billion a year;

b) impersonation of the dead is growing at a rate of 60% each year;

c) 77% of household waste contains at least one item which could assist fraudsters;

d) victims aged 31-40 (28%) are most likely to be repeat victims of an identity theft; and

e) nearly one in 10 Britons claim they have been the victim of identity fraud.

✓ ***"Man is least himself when he talks in his own person. Give him a mask, and he will tell you the truth" - Oscar Wilde***

BOOKS BASED ON LIES

The Boy Who Cried Wolf

A classic Aesop fable about a little boy who lied once too often and when he eventually told the truth no-one believed him (see page 29).

Burning Down My Master's House – My Life At the New York Times

"The New York Times" suffered one of its largest setbacks in its 152 year history in and around 2003 when one of its staff reporters, Jayson Blair, then aged 27, was found to have committed journalistic fraud. Blair duly resigned from the newspaper and in 2004 published the above book which told of his drug problems and his bipolar disorder.

During the investigation into Blair's work "The Times" found problems with at least 36 of the 73 articles and the newspaper actually published an e-mail address for readers to contact should they know of any other fabrications in Blair's work. One review of the book described Blair as a world-class Pinocchio.

The Confidence Man: His Masquerade

Written by Herman Melville, the author of "Moby Dick", this book was published on 1st April, 1857. The publication date was timed exactly to fall on 1st April as the plot of the book takes place on April Fool's Day on board a Mississippi steamship on its way to New Orleans.

✓ ***"Society can exist only on the basis that there is some amount of polished lying and that no one says exactly what he thinks" - Lin Yutang***

The book tells the story of a confidence trickster who sets out to defraud his fellow passengers. He assumes various guises and gets more enjoyment than money from his hoaxes. The enjoyment of hoaxing his fellow passengers seems to be an end in itself for the slippery con man. The interlocking tales of a group of passengers shows how the stranger tries to test their confidence and how each passenger is forced to face that in which he places his trust.

Con Man: A Master Swindler's Own Story
A co-written autobiography this book tells the story of Joseph "Yellow Kid" Weil who became a con man who is said to have stolen over eight million dollars. One of his favourite cons was the old wiretap scheme for horseplayers trying to beat the odds.

"The Cruise of the Kawa"
Published in 1921, this book relates the travels of Walter E Traprock around the South Pacific. Amongst his many discoveries was a bird which laid square eggs (see page 157).

The Double Cross System
A summary of some of the double cross operations during World War II written by J C Masterman. It tells the story of agents such as Snow and Zigzag and how they lived their double lives (see page 153).

✓ ***"The masses have never thirsted after truth. Whoever can supply them with illusions is easily their master; whoever attempts to destroy their illusions is always their victim" - Gustave Le Bon***

The Dirty War

Written by Martin Dillon this book delves into the real-life underground world of double and triple agents. It also uncovers some of the tactics used in political conflicts and reveals some of the dirty tricks, conspiracies, propaganda, and disinformation which were used by MI5 and MI6 (see page 152).

The Fabulist

In the 1990's Stephen Glass, at the age of 25, was the rising star of Washington journalism. In 2003 the American journalist, published a novel called "The Fabulist" telling the story of his lies as the associate editor of the political magazine "The New Republic". The book, with the tag line "a novel of an ignominious fall, the rise to infamy, and life after both", told the story of how he had managed to deceive his editor with fabricated stories over a 3 year period, and how he even created fake sources and websites to cover his tracks. Also in 2003 a film was made called "Shattered Glass" telling the same story.

The Great Salad Oil Swindle

Written by "Wall Street Journal" reporter Norman C Miller this is the true story of Tino De Angelis, a New York commodities broker who bought and sold vegetable oil futures around the world. In 1962 De Angelis began a huge scam to corner the soybean oil market.

At the end of the scam, 51 banks were left with debts of over $175 million. In 1964 Miller won a Pulitzer Prize for his reporting on the story (see page 97).

✓ ***"When people who are honestly mistaken learn the truth, they will either cease being mistaken, or cease being honest!" – Anonymous***

Ladystinger
A début novel by Craig Smith which was made into a film in 1993 film, staring Christopher Walken. The novel tells the story of a lady con-artist who scams the rich in Miami Beach. When she picks up the wrong mark he blackmails her into working with him on a scam in Jamaica which turns out to be deadly.

Lies and the Lying Liars Who Tell Them
Written by Al Franken in 2003, a comedian, political commentator and Senator, this is a satirical book about American politics. It put Fox News well and truly in the dock by using their tag line "Fair and Balanced".

Fox duly sued Franken for using the phrase which only served to increase the sales of the book. It also takes to task the Bush administration.

The Man Who Never Was
This is a true story about a great lie, written in 1953 by Ewen Montague, (and later made into a World War II war film staring Clifton Webb), and the elaborate plan by British Intelligence, entitled "Operation Mincemeat" to deceive the Axis powers into thinking that the allied invasion of Sicily would take place elsewhere.

The plan involved acquiring a dead body and giving it a false identity and fake letters saying that the Allied attack would be against Sardinia and Greece rather than Sicily and dropping the body in the sea off the coast of Spain. The plot was successful and the Germans completely believe the whole lie (see page 150).

✓ ***"The truth is not always beautiful, nor beautiful words the truth" – Lao Tzu***

Operation Mincemeat
The full story of "The Man Who Never Was" (see opposite) written by Ben Macintyre.

New York Sawed In Half
When two con men spread the rumour that Manhattan is sinking into the harbour mayhem quickly ensues. The two propose that Manhattan Island is sawed in half, towed out into the harbour and then turned round and brought back This legendary hoax was turned into a book called "New York Sawed in Half" by the American writer, Joel Rose, published by Bloomsbury in 2001 (see page 58).

It reveals the complicity which exists between the hoaxer and the hoaxed. "Vanity Fair" described the book as "a suspenseful saga which relives the greatest hoax ever recorded in New York City history."

Son of a Grifter: The Twisted Tale of Sante and Kenny Kimes, the Most Notorious Con Artists in America
The above autobiography by Kent Walker, the older son of Sante Kimes became a best seller and won the Edgar Allan Poe Award in 2002 (see page 107).

The Politics of Lying: Implications for Democracy
Written by Lionel Cliffe this book deals with the secrecy and deception of those in power. It includes a number of case-studies on foreign policy and international politics dealing with everything from security to the war on drugs. In its conclusion it discusses what can be done by democracies to be more open-minded and to have accountability by governments.

✓ ***"Excuses are always mixed with lies" - Arabian Proverb***

The Rise of Political Lying
Written by Peter Oborne, the Political Editor of "The Spectator" this book traces the history of political lying back to its origins. It shows how lying, or being "economical with the truth", has become almost acceptable and is part and parcel of modern day politics. From patchy announcements through to blatant falsehoods, Oborne shows how the political lie is always around and has led to such an enormous distrust of our politicians.

The Talented Mr Ripley
A novel by Patricia Highsmith is the story of a debonair confidence man who has a talent for self invention which eventually leads to murder. This was made into a film in 1998 starring Matt Damon, Jude Law and Gwyneth Paltrow.

Telling Lies: Clues to Deceit in the Marketplace, Politics and Marriage
This book, by a Professor of Psychology, Dr Paul Ekman, shows how different people lie and how to tell if they are lying. Whether breaking the law or breaking a promise it studies how people lie and how they can be caught.

The Tooth Fairy
Although there are several books about the Tooth Fairy, this one by Graham Joyce is very different. It tells the story of a seven year old boy, Sam Southall, who, on losing a tooth is visited by a sinister and demonic being whose influence spills over onto his family and friends.

✓ ***"Facing the truth is so much easier than all the time and energy it takes running away from it" - Sally Field***

FILMS BASED ON LIES

The Adventures of Baron Munchausen

This is a film made in 1988 which tells the story of the 18th century German born baron (pictured below) who tells outrageous, unbelievable stories, which he claims to be true. Munchausen had a reputation for his witty and exaggerated tales which were based on old folktales.

Note: The name "Munchausen" was given to describe a factitious syndrome in which patients will make up and simulate illnesses to gain attention, named after the man famous for telling wild and unbelievable stories.

Big Fat Liar

This is a classic case of "The Boy Who Cried Wolf." The story is about a 14 year old boy who cannot resist lying. One day he loses a story he has written for his homework and later finds out that the story has been turned into a movie. He then has to try and convince everyone that it is his story and goes to see the producer of the film who also turns out to be a compulsive liar.

✓ ***"Men occasionally stumble over the truth, but most of them pick themselves up and hurry off as if nothing had happened" - Winston Churchill***

Catch Me If You Can
This 2002 film, staring Leonard de Caprio, tells the true story of Frank Abagnale Jr, an American born 1948 who, as a teenager, was a successful confidence trickster, cheque forger and impostor and posed as a Pan Am pilot, doctor and a lawyer (see page 88).

Abagnale now works as a security consultant and has his own company which advises businesses on how to deal with fraud. He has become a millionaire through his various consultancies and continues to advise the FBI with whom he has been associated for over 35 years.

Dirty Rotten Scoundrels
A 1998 film about two fraudsters living on the French Riviera who try and con money out of rich women. They meet one day on a train and try to work together but soon realise there is only enough "work" for one. They come to an agreement that the first one to successfully con one young woman out of $50,000 will stay in town and the other will have to leave.

I Love You Phillip Morris
Jim Carey stared in this film which was nominated for a Best Comedy Award in 2011. Based on the real life story of Steve Russell, played by Jim Carey, who turns to cons and fraud which see him land in jail (see page 93). There he meets the love of his life, Phillip Morris, played by Ewan McGregor, and so starts a sequence of escapes and confidence tricks as he tries to ensure a lavish lifestyle for himself and his fellow inmate on their release from prison.

✓ ***"There are many lies but barely one truth" - Ukranian Proverb***

Fooling Hitler
With the tagline, 'the true story of the greatest deception of World War II", this epic story, starring Jason Durr, tells how a group of writers, artists and technicians set out to fool German High Command. Code named "Operation Bodyguard" the group proved that, by the deception of setting up decoy airfields, soldiers, guns, and inflatable tanks just before D Day, they could suggest that an invasion would take place in Calais rather than Normandy. General Patton was placed in charge of this "invasion force" which successfully convinced Hitler that another invasion would take place in Calais.

At the end of the war various maps and documents were discovered which showed that Hitler believed the subterfuge of Patton's invisible army of 2 million men.

The Hoax
This film, starring Richard Gere, told the true story of writer Clifford Irving who, in an audacious hoax sold a bogus biography of Howard Hughes to the publishers, McGraw Hill, and so created a great media frenzy (see page 68).

When the film was made Irving had already spent 17 months in prison and had published a book about the whole incident, also called "The Hoax."

In a bizarre twist, Irving ridiculed the film saying it was a distortion of the story and "a hoax about a hoax." The film earned Richard Gere the "Actor of Year" award in 2007.

✓ ***"Truth never penetrates an unwilling mind" - J. L. Borges***

The Invention of Lying
A 2009 romantic comedy staring Ricky Gervais living in a world where there are no lies and everyone tells the truth.

Gervais plays the part of a screenwriter who, on the spur of the moment, blurts out the very first lie. He lies to the teller at the bank saying that he has $800 in his account. The computer, however, says that he has only $300 in the account. The teller gives Gervais the full $800 anyway assuming the computer has made a mistake as no-one tells a lie. The film then goes on to test the discovery of lying.

Liar, Liar
In this film Jim Carrey plays a lawyer who is always breaking promises to his son. On the son's seventh birthday the child blows out his candles and makes a wish that his father will stop lying for just 24 hours. The wish comes true and Jim Carrey finds himself in a series of embarrassing situations because he finds he cannot lie.

The Man Who Never Was
(see page 176)

The Producers
This Mel Brooks film made in 1968 (re-made in 2005) – which later became a very successful musical – is an American black comedy and concerns two theatrical producers who devise a get-rich-quick scheme by overselling interests in a big flop and then plan to abscond to Brazil after opening night. The show unexpectedly turns out to be a success.

✓ ***"The truth is more important than the facts" - Frank Lloyd Wright***

Quiz Show
A young lawyer in the late 1950's discovers that a TV quiz show is being fixed.

Based on a real live scandal, it tells the story of how Columbia University instructor, Charles van Doren, rose to fame as a contestant on the show. Directed by Robert Redford with Ralph Fiennes in the role of van Doren it shows how week after week people tuned in to see van Doren win, little realizing that he was being fed the answers.

Scam
A 1993 film, staring Christopher Walken, adapted from a novel by Craig Smith entitled "Ladystinger" (see page 176). A con-artist scams the rich in Miami Beach. When she picks up the wrong mark he blackmails her into working with him on a scam in Jamaica which turns out to be deadly.

Shattered Glass
Another American journalist, Stephen Glass who became famous for his lies, was the 25 year old associate editor of the political magazine "The New Republic". In the 1990's Glass, who was the rising star of Washington journalism not only managed to deceive his editor with fabricated stories over a 3 year period he even created fake sources and websites to cover his tracks.

Five years after his dismissal a feature film about the whole episode called "Shattered Glass" was released in 2003 starring Hayden Christensen with the tagline "He would do anything just to get a great story."

✓ ***"Truth, must of necessity be stranger than fiction; for we have made fiction to suit ourselves" – G. K. Chesterton***

Glass also published a book called "The Fabulist" (see page 175) telling his own story.

The Sting

Staring Robert Redford and Paul Newman, "The Sting" is a 1973 film set in 1930's Chicago inspired by the con men Fred and Charley Gondorff.

A young con man seeks revenge for the murder of his partner by a gang working for a criminal banker. He teams up with the master of the big con and so gets his revenge by winning a fortune from the said banker.

The title means the moment when the con man has taken the victim's money and has disappeared before the victim realises he has been cheated.

The Talented Mr Ripley

Based on a novel by Patricia Highsmith (see page 178) and staring Matt Damon, Jude Law and Gwyneth Paltrow.

✓ ***"The best ammunition against lies is the truth - there is no ammunition against gossip. It is like a fog and the clear wind blows it away and the sun burns it off" - Ernest Hemingway***

TV PROGRAMMES BASED ON LIES

Call My Bluff

This was a long running TV game show where two teams of three took it in turns to give three definition of an obscure word. Only one definition was correct and the other team had to decide who was telling the truth. As the words were so outlandish any of the three definitions could have been correct.

Although the show only lasted six months in America, it proved much more popular in England and the BBC ran the successful programme from 1965–1988 and then again from 1996–2005. A book about the programme called (surprisingly enough!) "Call My Bluff" was published in 1972 by Frank Muir and Patrick Campbell.

Lie to Me

An American TV series, staring Tim Roth who plays Dr Cal Lightman, the world's leading deception expert which premiered in 2009. The publicity called Lightman "a human lie detector." The show is about a group of psychologists who help the police in their investigations by applied psychology and what was called facial action coding and body language. Based on real-life scientific discoveries of psychologist, Paul Ekman, the series follows the group of deception experts as they uncover the truth behind the lies.

✓ ***"Some people will not tolerate such emotional honesty in communication. They would rather defend their dishonesty on the grounds that it might hurt others. Therefore, having rationalized their phoniness into nobility, they settle for superficial relationships" - Author Unknown***

"On the Run" King of Con

The true story of career criminal Steven Jay Russell as he escapes from Harris County prison, Texas, for the third time. Con man Russell also known as "King Con" is currently serving a 144 year jail sentence for being a long established con man who also made a series of amazing jail breaks (see page 93).

The Real Hustle

This is a factual programme and features a team of hustlers who work a series of scams on members of the public. Usually the victims have been set up by their families and the object is to show how to avoid such scams in real life. At the end of the programme any money or property which has been taken is returned to them and their permission obtained to broadcast their scam.

Hustle

This drama series follows a group of con artists who pull off deceptions on "fat cat" businessmen etc and try to redress the balance in a kind of Robin Hood way. The programme, first broadcast in 2004, is now in its seventh series and stars Adrian Lester, Robert Glenister, Robert Vaughn and Matt Di Angelo. The slogan of the programme is "The con is on."

Yes Virginia, There Is A Santa Clause

From the famous original story this was adapted in 1991 into a made for TV movie with Charles Bronson as the famous editor, Francis Church (see page 30).

✓ ***"Ye shall know the truth, and the truth shall make you mad" - Aldous Huxley***

Would I lie to you?

This is a BBC comedy panel show where each member of the panel has to try and bluff the others about their deepest secrets.

✓ ***"Do not fear to repeat what has already been said. Men need the truth dinned into their ears many times and from all sides. The first rumour makes them prick up their ears, the second registers, and the third enters" - Rene Laennec***

LIES ON THE RADIO

No Lies Radio
Broadcast every weekday from San Francisco the No Lies Radio is heard world-wide. It is a mixture of music, talk shows and news and people are encouraged to 'phone in with their views on practically any subject.

War of the Worlds
The above play by H G Wells was supposed to have caused widespread panic when it was broadcast in 1938 but some people believe that the story about the panic was more of a hoax than the story itself. Written in 1898 the play was one episode in an anthology series. More than half the play, performed on Halloween, was presented as a series of "news bulletins" told of an actual alien invasion by Martians which was currently in progress. The fact that the play ran without commercial breaks only added to the realism (left - cover of the first edition of the book).

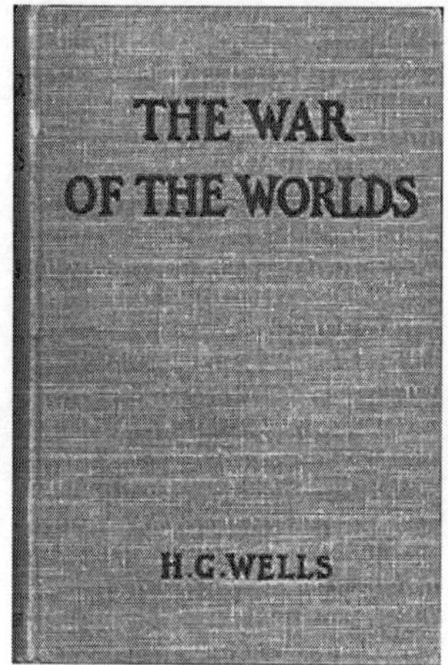

Directed and narrated by Wells, the format of the play was later decried as being cruelly deceptive.

✓ ***"We tell lies when we are afraid - afraid of what we don't know, afraid of what others will think, afraid of what will be found out about us. But every time we tell a lie, the thing that we fear grows stronger" - Tad Williams***

GAMES BASED ON LIES

Truth or Lies
A party game for up to eight players answering a huge range of thought-provoking questions. The game is said to be able to pick up stress levels in your voice to detect whether you are telling the truth or not.

The Lying Game
Each player has to write down three things about themselves, two of which are lies. In turn each player reads out their statements and the others have to guess which one is true. Each time a player guesses the right answer they gain a point and if no one guesses the right answer then the liar gains points. At the end of the game the player with the most points is the winner.

The "Lying King" Storytelling Game
Similar to "The Lying Game", each child takes it in turn to tell a story to the Lying King. If the Lying King thinks the story is false he will roar, if he thinks the story is true he will say "naah". If the King is right he gets a point, and if the King is wrong then the storyteller gets a point. The game ends with the first player to get three points.

Liars' Dice Game
Played by two or more players this game is based on guesses and lies. A screen is placed between the players as they roll five dice each. They then make a claim saying what the five dice are but they do not have to tell the truth and their opponents have to gamble on whether they are telling the truth or not.

✓ ***"To see what is in front of one's nose requires a constant struggle" - George Orwell***

THE WORLD'S BIGGEST LIAR COMPETION

Each November a competition is held in west Cumbria for the world's biggest liar. Competitors from all over the world gather to serve up tall stories with a pot supper.

Inspired by the tall tales of Will Ritson (picture right) (1808-1890) the competition is held in his memory. Ritson, the landlord of the Wastwater Hotel (now called the Wasdale Heade Inn), was a great story teller. One of the tales which he said was quite true was that he found a wounded eagle near the inn and nursed it back to health and kept it in his chicken coop. One night a bitch hound got into the coop and five months later the dog gave birth to a litter of winged hounds!

There are very few rules to the competition but perhaps the most interesting is the fact that politicians and lawyers are unable to take part as they are too professional! The stories must be not longer than three minutes, and no notes or props are allowed. Many strange and wonderful stories have been told during the course of the competition the latest one being that the mountains and lakes of Essex were stolen by Cumbrians leaving Essex a dull and flat landscape!

✓ ***"If at first you don't succeed, lie, lie again" - Laurence J. Peter***

INDEX

Pearl Bramble was born and brought up in Lincolnshire. It was when she went to work in London that she met her husband and they went off to work in South Africa. On their return they lived in Hertfordshire for a few years where they had twins – a boy and a girl. When the twins were four years of age the family packed up and went to live and work in Australia for two years. On returning they settled in Leigh on Sea, Essex where Pearl and her husband have now lived for more than 30 years. After working as a legal secretary in the City, Pearl retired. She then worked for five years in a volunteer organization writing and producing a volunteers' magazine. This is her first book.

All images are taken from Wikipedia and are in the public domain because the copyright has expired.

June 2011..(C)